Timis

THE GLORY OF HIS PRESENCE

Also by Lois and Ken Gott

The Sunderland Refreshing

The Glory of His Presence

Reaping the Harvest of the Sunderland Refreshing

Lois Gott

Hodder & Stoughton
LONDON SYDNEY AUCKLAND

British Library Cataloguing in Publication Data
A record for this book is available from the British Library

ISBN 0 340 67867 4

Typeset by Hewer Text Composition Services, Edinburgh
Printed and bound in Great Britain by
Cox & Wyman Ltd, Reading, Berks.

Hodder and Stoughton Ltd
A Division of Hodder Headline PLC
338 Euston Road
London NW1 3BH

Contents

Preface

I have just returned from a visit to the Sunderland Christian Centre in England, where God is doing a most unusual work of his grace. Whilst there I had the opportunity to share with many of the leaders and workers of the church and found a most unique mix of people all committed to, and enjoying the renewing work of the Holy Spirit in their lives. As I sat and assessed what I saw, I came to the conclusion that there was a distinct work of God taking place in this church, and many of the ingredients required for revival were beginning to be seen amongst them.

Sunderland itself is a city of no great appeal. There have, however, been previous revival moves within its borders, and the people are most conscious of this heritage. Ken and Lois Gott are the senior pastors of what has become a significant and growing Assemblies of God church. It is apparent that they have been radically touched and transformed by this present blessing. They demonstrate an absolute dependence on the Holy Spirit, and it leaves its impression on all who come into contact with them. I believe the following key ingredients of revival can be seen at work in this church.

A Spirit of Love – From the moment you step into the church you are overwhelmed by the love of God amongst his people.

A Spirit of Humility – They all know that it is nothing of their own doing. It is only God's favour upon them.

A Spirit of Grace – They allow so much freedom in their services. People feel able to express themselves unreservedly.

A Spirit of Unity – Leaders and people from all over Europe and beyond meet together under the common banner of Christ's love.

A Spirit of Reconciliation – There is a genuine desire to see the body of Christ made whole. National and denominational prejudices are repented of, and great scenes of weeping and restoration are common.

A Spirit of Joy – This joyfulness invades everything they do. It is not only in the services but all through their daily lives together. These people are enjoying God's presence.

A Spirit of Giving – There is a generous spirit in every area of their church life and ministries. While I was there, a man had the wheels of his car stolen during one of the services. Immediately an offering was taken and the giving greatly exceeded the cost of the wheels. Their generosity extends far beyond finances and has become a way of life for this church.

A Spirit of Faith – You cannot help but become a part of the vision of this unique church. They are not content to camp around this spring of refreshing, but rather are committed to yet greater expressions of faith and service. New magazines, television programmes, youth outreaches, new churches, conferences, missions trips, new facilities, all come to the surface during a conversation with any of the church's leaders.

A Spirit of Rest – If God doesn't do it, it doesn't happen. There is a wonderful awesome simplicity found in the functioning of this church. They have learnt, and are learning what it is to enter into a place of divine rest, where the Holy Spirit is allowed to conduct his business as he wishes.

A Spirit of Security – You feel safe in this place. Much happens as God's Spirit moves upon his people, and yet at no time did I ever feel as though there was a lack of direction or government in the place. I felt more secure to allow the Holy Spirit to touch my life in this place than in any other I have visited.

God is at work in Sunderland, England, just as he is all over the nations. However, there is much we can learn from this unique body of people, as they seek to follow the Holy Spirit into yet deeper waters of renewal and revival.

Steve Penny
Executive Member of Assemblies of God
Brisbane, Australia

Foreword

The first time I met Lois Gott was in a coffee shop in Toronto, Canada. My husband, Andrew, and I had just finished a meal with some friends when we noticed Ken Gott at a nearby table. Andrew had met him a few months earlier during a time of ministry that had knit their hearts together in a special way. But this time Lois was with him and Ken quickly made the introductions. Lois and I exchanged a warm hug and then she immediately declared that our meeting was a divine appointment! She told me that before she and Ken left England the Lord dropped my name into her heart as someone to come to Sunderland to minister to the ladies in their church. Before I could catch my breath Lois extended an invitation to me.

It was no surprise that I felt immediately drawn to Lois since Andrew and I already felt deeply connected in the Spirit with her husband Ken. However, I quickly informed her that although I would love to come, the Lord had me on a sabbatical season of rest and I was not accepting any invitations. Besides, I hadn't been to Great Britain since 1982 and didn't know when I might return.

For the next several days in Toronto we had rich fellowship with the Gotts. We left not knowing exactly when we'd see them again, but we knew that we would. As it turned out, within a few months Andrew and I made a very unexpected trip to England. It was the perfect opportunity to visit Ken and Lois and continue to nurture the deep bond of relationship we felt with them. When they asked us to minister in their church we felt honored and gladly accepted. And so we ended up in Sunderland after all.

Today, when I think of the Gotts and Sunderland Christian Centre, I wonder why there aren't more places on earth where Christians are willing to live the Gospel the way the Bible describes it. Jesus said in Matthew 25, '*For I was hungry, and you gave me something to eat; I was thirsty, and you gave me drink; I was a stranger, and you invited me in; naked, and you clothed me; I was sick, and you visited me; I was in prison, and you came to me . . . Truly I say to you, to the extent that you did it to one of these brothers of mine, even the least of them, you did it to me.*'

Ken and Lois and their Sunderland congregation are *doing* it. They have filled themselves with the love and compassion of God and they are taking it out to the streets. Out to the hungry ones, the castaways, the criminals, the sick, the lonely and the brokenhearted. They are showing God's love in its simplest yet most potent form. I am not at all surprised that the Lord is responding with increased favour, a growing church and a powerful outpouring of His precious Holy Spirit.

Ken and Lois Gott have not discovered some new secret formula for success. To the contrary, they are just following the blueprint God gave in His word. And when anyone follows it, results will follow. Of course, it takes humility to lay down your own plan and follow someone else's, even when that someone else is God. But Ken and Lois are marked by a genuine humility that is precious in God's sight. They are truly amazed at what God is doing in their midst and I have never heard them hesitate to give Him all the credit. They are kind and unassuming, yet mighty in spirit, strong in conviction and fierce in spiritual battle. They have to be. They are on the front lines.

If there were more leaders like the Gotts and more churches like Sunderland Christian Centre, reaching the world with the love of Jesus would come more naturally and with greater joy for all of us. This book is a remarkable collection of inspiring stories that are certain to raise your level of faith. I hope by reading it you will be encouraged to open your heart to more of the Lord's love for you and for the lost and, in doing so, be inspired to open more of your church, your home and your heart to the lost and hurting of this world.

God is not looking for people with big names. He simply wants people with big hearts. That is what He found in Ken and Lois Gott. Andrew and I count it a privilege to be called their friends. They have inspired us. We have seen yet another wonderful aspect of the heart of Jesus reflected in their lives and in their ministry.

Melody Green Sievright
Co-Founder of Last Days Ministries

Introduction

Many of you may have read our story recounted in the book *The Sunderland Refreshing*. It tells of the events surrounding the wonderful visitation of the Holy Spirit we experienced beginning in August 1994. For nineteen months we held services every evening in our church, Sunderland Christian Centre, for literally thousands who have come to visit from all around the world and experience this new move of the Holy Spirit. Because of the volume of people attending our church from all denominations and all nations it has drawn much media attention. God had put the church back on the map. We found the world to be a much smaller, kinder and gloriously loving place as visitors became friends, walls of hostility and division came down, and the body of Christ came together.

We felt the writing of this book was incredibly important since the question has been posed to us many times, 'What is the fruit of all you have been experiencing?' Others have asked, 'Well, where do we go from here?' We would not presume to have all the answers, but this book chronicles our journey moving from renewal into a wonderful harvest. Incredible salvation testimonies among major criminal figures are recounted alongside stories of miraculous healings. The prayer strategy for taking a city, taught to us by the Argentinians experiencing revival in their own country, runs alongside the accounts of God's Spirit changing the lives of our community. This book has been written for all those who might ask, 'What now? Where do we go from here?' and to encourage all, with miraculous stories of the power of God at work today.

Over the last few months we have been inspired by the history of the Salvation Army. As you read this book you will see many references to the great General William Booth. What has been happening to us here in Sunderland echoes many of those early turn-of-the-century experiences. God has changed our hearts. We have been made aware of our destiny. He's looking to send labourers into his harvest field. In Sunderland we have found the river of God running into the poor communities, into the hostels for the homeless, in the street gangs, into the lives of the alcoholics and the no-hopers. What we have experienced has been nothing short of miraculous, and we believe it is only the beginning. I hope you will find many of those things shared both helpful and inspiring.

Chapter 1

Kissed a Guilty World

'Missus, have you got a hanky?' Lesley, head buried in the collar of her thick winter coat, stopped abruptly. Peering around in the gloom, eyes stung by the biting wind, she wondered where the cry had come from. For eight years she had walked to work as our church secretary, yet on this particular morning God was about to speak suddenly and powerfully to us again.

Searching around in the gloom as faded derelict buildings loomed into view, Lesley thought she must have been mistaken. However, more urgently this time she heard the cry, 'Missus, have you got a hanky?' Cautiously she began to make her way up a darkened alley-way stepping gingerly over debris, bricks and stones. This was a place of utter squalor reeking of decay. It was with some amusement she noted that these were the very run-down shop units which once housed our church office years before. A small figure crouched in the corner, unsuccessfully attempting to keep out the cold. His nose streamed and his knees bled. Moving closer, Lesley could see that he was no more than eight years old. Overcome with compassion she knelt there in the filth to gently wipe the runny nose and attend to his bleeding limbs.

'Why aren't you in school?' she asked.

'I've been bad[1] and me mam's kept us off school, but she's gone out and told us not to go back till five o'clock.'

Lesley glanced down at her watch which read 9.30 a.m., seven and a half hours to wait. Gently cleaning him up she urged him to stay where he was so that she could have someone attend to him immediately. Wiping a tear from her eye she turned to run to the office and a telephone.

'Missus, missus.' She heard the piercing cry again and turned once more to face him. 'Missus, can you give us a kiss?' he asked. Eyes overflowing with tears, Lesley stumbled back up the alley and, bending over the crouched figure, kissed his cold little cheek.

Later that day the Holy Spirit spoke powerfully to my own heart. For over a year we had been involved in an extraordinary move of God. During this time the Father had been, figuratively speaking, kissing us, his people, with love. We had been falling in love with the Lord Jesus Christ all over again. Now, however, I had been powerfully prompted that it was time to kiss a broken and needy world with the love by which we had been kissed.

Our hearts had been enlarged. To reach the world was no longer merely a Christian duty or furtherance of my own empire, or numbers in a church building. Our good works had been replaced in the last year by hearts truly overwhelmed with love for the down-trodden and oppressed, the sick and the sinner. The Father's gentle wooing of his bride had caused us to truly love the unlovely and weep for a lost and broken world. Weeping before the Lord that day on my knees, I was aware that one little

1. 'bad': northeastern slang meaning ill or sick.

boy was about to lead us out into the streets. This world needed the kiss of Jesus.

As I knelt, the words of a verse of that old Welsh hymn resounded in my ears.

> On the mount of crucifixion
> Fountains opened deep and wide;
> Through the floodgates of God's mercy
> Flowed a vast and gracious tide.
>
> Grace and love like mighty rivers,
> Poured incessant from above,
> Heaven's peace and perfect justice
> Kissed a guilty world in love.[2]

As General Booth had been moved at the end of the nineteenth century by the plight of the poor and needy of his community and propelled into action, we were now ourselves deeply affected by the world around us. Those great awakenings of old, times of spiritual revival in the Church, had gone on to produce a mighty harvest of souls beginning with those most needy, poor and bound. From a Holy Ghost invasion came an explosion of Christian witness and love. We had in Sunderland been kissed by God's love and were now about to kiss the world with the love of the Father.

---

2. 'Here is love vast as the ocean', Henry T. Smart, copyright anon.

Chapter 2

God Can Do It Here

'More, Lord,' cried the group of visitors from Adelaide, Australia, as they stood to their feet to receive prayer. How often we had heard those words over the last year, and yet I had a sense in my spirit that, we having 'tarried in our Jerusalem' until we were filled with power from on high, the Lord was about to thrust us into the harvest-field. A local Catholic priest, born again and Spirit-filled, stepped forward to lay hands on them. With cries and shouts, laughter and tears, all fell to the floor overcome by the Holy Spirit.

More people of obviously varying nationalities streamed forward, hungry to receive a fresh touch of the Spirit in their lives. I gazed upwards into the vast expanse of the roof in our church building and my heart joined with the prayer being offered, 'Lord, give us burning hearts and make us shining lights in this world of darkness.' Once again I was both amazed and moved by the ongoing scene before me. An Anglican priest joined by a Salvation Army captain moved forward to help minister to the many visitors as my husband remained in his seat unobserved in his own church. In my heart there was no longer a need to be seen or heard. For him, as an Assemblies of God Pentecostal pastor, such interdenominational co-operation more than a year ago would have seemed impossible. How great a work of grace God had accomplished in our hearts during this period of renewal. Rather than competing in hostility and suspicion as we had once done, we were working together honouring and preferring one another in love.

For over a year we had been holding services six nights every week in this unlikely venue deep in the East End of Sunderland. The so-called 'Toronto Blessing' marked by unusual manifestations had arrived in Sunderland in August 1994. Thousands of hearts and lives had been profoundly changed now that we had a new passion for Jesus. So many had been the visitors that even our local Pizza Hut restaurant had run out of dough and been forced to close early! Local and national newspapers ran stories of the huge number of visitors from all over the world arriving to worship at an insignificant little church.

When Ken and I returned from the Toronto Airport Vineyard Church that August, impacted by God in a life-changing way, we never dreamt that over a year later we would still be ministering to hundreds each evening. Denominations had come together, lives were forever changed. Personally I no longer felt the need to perform and had relinquished the drive to succeed in my ministry. My only desire was a greater intimacy with God my Father. In every single service we had urged people not to focus on the manifestations they would see but to be good fruit inspectors and to examine the fruit in individual lives as they gave public testimony. There had been some wonderful fruit!

Jim Richardson, a well-known local gangster, had during the past year turned from a life of crime to loving and serving the Lord Jesus Christ with all his heart. In fact, so profound was the change he is now engaged in full-time ministry in running kids off the street and into the kingdom of God.

Denise Wilson, one of our office staff whose family had been dramatically transformed during the past year, has been used by the Lord to facilitate a wonderful and extraordinary healing resulting in members of a family finding Christ as their personal saviour.

A harvest of souls had now become a burning passion in my heart and daily our faith was growing. That which was being accomplished for God in other nations in terms of full-scale revival we increasingly believed was possible here. Ken and I continually reminded ourselves of a prophecy given by Dave Roberts, then editor of *Alpha* magazine. While in John and Carol Arnott's home in Toronto, he saw us in a vision walking through a door into a vast harvest-field. Nothing less than a harvest of souls was our one desire. A river of humanity coming to Christ had to be the fruit of all we were engaged in.

There was so much fruit in the lives of my own wonderful people in the church here in Sunderland it was difficult to quantify. Godly Christian men and women had so tirelessly given and given again to humbly serve visitors from all over the world. Not only had they adapted to a lifestyle of protracted meetings but our own local church had more than doubled. Finding room for the whole congregation and space for them all to park their vehicles is a major problem. In order to ease the pressure, three weeks out of four we decided to meet in separate venues.

Our whole leadership structure has of necessity been revolutionised because of the sudden growth. The most amazing evidence of grace and humility being worked in lives was to be seen when leaders of long standing laid down their former positions in order to make way for a new team. Men's gifts and ministries were acknowledged with a love that made these new structures possible.

Now our church leadership team included a man that little over a year ago we didn't even know, a Brethren local family doctor. Truthfully, before God's Spirit was poured out in our lives we could never have come together. Now we rejoice in those things that bring us to unity, not in those that divide. God has added to us a Bible teacher of the highest calibre and a man of character and integrity.

It was with joy that we sent out a team of ordinary men and women to Albania on a ministry trip. An excited pastor phoned to tell us that he has seen two hundred new converts added to his church in the three months following the visit. The harvest is still going on today. God is releasing the whole body of Christ to ministry. Men and women, who had until recently only filled church pews, carried the presence of God with them to the town of Kuchove and revival was the result.

My father, Herbert Harrison, has been a minister in the Assemblies of God Pentecostal Church for forty-seven years. A statesman in his own right, he and his wife Mary had been radically changed during this outpouring of the Spirit. In fact they were set on fire with a new passion for Jesus. With a growing conviction I knew that though he was in his seventy-third year he would be instrumental in helping to move what was happening in the church into the streets. After all, had his whole life not been solely motivated to see the lost won for the Father?

Because we as a church family shared that desire, just as the people had generously sent Ken and me to Toronto to receive all God had for us, in the same way they

7

honoured Herbert and Mary with a visit to Argentina. There a refreshing of the Holy Spirit had moved into full-scale revival. We were thrilled to hear of churches open twenty-three hours a day to facilitate service after service for the thousands of converts. How I chuckled when I heard this. All we in Sunderland thought we had stretched so far to accommodate services every evening. How would we cope with services twenty-three hours of the day? I honestly didn't know but I did know we were willing!

New paths were about to open to us far sooner than expected . . .

Chapter 3

Love for the Lost

We had always known the principle of reaching the lost for the Father and had been a church with an excellent evangelistic edge. Our 'Sunday at Six' services had followed the 'Willow Creek' model.[1] Every Sunday evening we staged a relevant gospel presentation for the unchurched, with some success. Even so I knew that we had planned programmes but lacked the one essential, the power of the living God. We had strategised, organised and been full of activity but seen little fruit in proportion to all our man-made plans.

Now I was very much aware of the fact that the Father had come to us in an unusual and unexpected way. We had fallen on the floor, laughed, cried, experienced all manner of phenomena, yet more importantly our hearts burst with love for God and love for the lost. God had been enlisting his army in love. He had trusted us with an awesome responsibility. Jesus said, 'As my Father has sent me . . . even so send I you.' 'A love for the lost' had been

1. Willow Creek Church's 'seeker-sensitive' approach to evangelism uses contemporary methods, such as drama, but is carefully designed to be culturally relevant.

for many of us religious rhetoric, but now it was a real experience, a direct result of God's emotions being shared in our human hearts. The Father was not about to lead us into pleasant places and to popular people, but to dark and desperate areas. We often aren't aware of mankind's needs and pains until tragedy intrudes into our own lives. However, we now knew we had the enabling power of the Holy Spirit to go and preach the gospel.

The Lord had come as told in Matthew 21 and turned over the tables of our practices and had begun to make our house a house of prayer. Scripture encourages us to believe that 'the blind would see, the deaf would hear, the gospel would be preached to the poor, the lame would walk, lepers be cleansed, the dead even raised to life'.

It was impossible not to think of the great man, General William Booth, whose meetings saw equally strange phenomena. In May 1879 the *Newcastle Chronicle* covered the story of an all-night Salvation Army meeting. The correspondent was not altogether sympathetic but after describing the hall, the participants and the singing, he continued:

This chorus might have been sung perhaps a dozen times when there was a shrill scream, a bustle around the platform, and a general rise of the audience. Seats were mounted; hands were raised in the air; the singing was mingled with loud 'hallelujahs', bursts of vociferous prayer, shouting and hysterical laughter. To add to the confusion, four of the forms fell backwards and threw their occupants into the common heap on the floor. So great was the commotion in the centre of the room, so terrifying was the din, that this incident, which would have thrown an ordinary congregation into uproar, passed almost unnoticed. Sinners were creeping to the penitent form; the Salvation Army was rejoicing; fully one-third of those present acted as if they were more or less insane. Several figures were bent double near the platform, groaning and wringing their hands.

However, this same General was seized by the love of God shed abroad in his heart to reach the world. Walking up the Mile End Road in London's East End, he had been so moved when seeing poor mothers feeding their babies gin, in order to stop their desperate cries because of their hunger pangs, that he declared, 'Truly I have found my destiny.'

William Booth and his wife, Catherine, founded the Salvation Army in 1865 in their home country, England. His passion for the lost, especially those who were considered 'irredeemable' by the established Church, was legendary. His whole life can be summed up in his own words, 'Go for souls – and go for the worst!'

The early Salvation Army set out to salvage souls of 'forgotten and forsaken' men and women. With a zeal unsurpassed by any, they declared 'salvation war' first in the London slums, then all over Europe, and eventually in every inhabited continent on earth. Theirs was a message of repentance and holiness unto the Lord. On every flag and banner was their insignia with the awesome words 'Blood and Fire!' As God moved in our own church it was to the 'irredeemable forgotten and forsaken' that we were drawn.

I also thought of John Wesley, probably the most well known of all revival preachers. Wesley, a brilliant Oxford Fellow and lecturer, was converted at thirty-five and went on to become the founder of the Methodist movement. He travelled over two hundred and fifty thousand miles on horseback, preached over forty thousand sermons and wrote five thousand sermons, tracts or pamphlets of some kind. John's brother, Charles, a partner in the work, wrote over sixty-five thousand hymns! Together they were used of God to transform the English world in their own lifetimes. John Wesley experienced all the same phenomena in his meetings that are taking place today.

In April 1739, Wesley preached at Newgate Prison in Bristol. Wesley records that as he was preaching, 'one, and another, and another sunk to the earth: they dropped on every side as thunderstruck. One of them cried aloud. We besought God on her behalf and He turned her heaviness into joy. A second being in the same agony, we called upon God for her also; and He spoke peace unto her soul.'[2]

Throughout his life Wesley witnessed such incredible revival phenomena that even though his preaching was the tool God was using, he was continually amazed. In one entry in his journal (on 29 July 1759), Wesley records a number of examples that occurred while preaching. 'Several fell to the ground, some of whom seemed dead, others in the agonies of death, the violence of their bodily convulsions exceeding all description. A child, seven years old, sees many visions and astonishes the neighbours with her innocent awful manner of declaring them.'[3]

Describing the same meeting, he details how the power of God moved out into the churchyard. The people were affected in ways that were beyond what he could describe. One man was 'wounded by the Lord' and while others tried to hold him up,

2. Patrick Dixon, *Signs of Revival* (Kingsway, 1994).
3. Dixon, *Signs of Revival*.

his own shaking exceeded that of a cloth in the wind. It seemed as if the Lord came upon him like a giant, taking him by the neck and shaking all his bones in pieces. Another roared and screamed. Some continued long as if they were dead, but with a calm sweetness in their looks. I saw one who lay two or three hours in the open air, and, being then carried into the house, continued insensible another hour, as if actually dead.[4]

So despised was Wesley in the established Church that he was forced into the fields and streets, preaching mostly to the poor working men. He was used to powerfully affect the nation and many believe that he saved Britain from a similar revolution to the French.

Then there was Evan Roberts – a man literally obsessed by desire for revival. His meetings, it was said, had the power to purify many drunken, lazy and lustful communities. Thousands and thousands went to their knees in repentance, among them big hard-skinned miners. Many publicans actually went bankrupt. There was chaos in the mines because the pit ponies could not understand the purified language of their masters The police found that they had no crimes to investigate. God was clearly at work.

For those of us at the forefront of the move of God in Sunderland it was clear that once again the Lord had brought to his church a new awakening. His Spirit was profoundly changing our lives. Now we needed to carry this to the desperate world around us. Each and every one of us carries his presence.

4. Dixon, *Signs of Revival*.

Chapter 4

Carriers of His Presence

God took hold of the life of Smith Wigglesworth, an illiterate Bradford plumber, in the revival of 1907 and used him to carry his presence around the world. Today, in this fresh awakening, God is looking for an army of millions who will do the same. It's the day of God's Spirit on all flesh. The Bible teaches us over and over again that God loves to bless the humble. The reason is simple. At all times and in every circumstance glory must go to God. No-one is ever born naturally humble. Humility is a garment we need to put on continually. 1 Peter 5:5–6 tells us,

> Young men, in the same way be submissive to those who are older. All of you, clothe yourselves with humility towards one another, because, 'God opposes the proud but gives grace to the humble.' Humble yourselves, therefore, under God's mighty hand, that he may lift you up in due time.

F.B. Meyer, the great Bible teacher, once said, 'I used to think that God's gifts were on shelves one above the other; and that the taller we grew in Christian character the easier we could reach them. I now find that God's gifts are on shelves one beneath the other. It is not a question of growing taller but of stooping lower; that we have to go down, always down to get His best gifts.'[1]

Charles Finney, the revivalist, travelled by train from one city to another to preach the gospel. As his carriage passed through each city, people would fall to the floor under the power of God and cry out in repentance under conviction of sin. Such was the presence of God he carried.

The Bible tells us of the apostle Peter. So heavy was the anointing of the presence of God upon his life that, even as his shadow fell across the sick, they were instantly healed. In this day of the gracious outpouring of the Holy Spirit we need, like those apostles, to be carriers of his presence – carriers of his presence in the supermarkets, carriers of his presence in the workplace, carriers of his presence in our streets and neighbourhoods, carriers of his presence in the hospitals, carriers of his presence in the prisons. We need to be so full of the power of the Holy Spirit that we can affect our world wherever we choose to go.

2 Samuel 6:1–12 recounts an incident of how we shouldn't and how we should carry the presence of God.

David again brought together out of Israel chosen men, thirty thousand in all. He and all his men set out from Baalah of Judah to bring up from there the ark of God, which is called by the Name, the name of the Lord Almighty, who is enthroned between the cherubim that are on the ark. They set the ark of God on a new cart and brought it from the house of Abinadab, which was

1. *Bible Illustrator for Windows.*

on the hill. Uzzah and Ahio, sons of Abinadab, were guiding the new cart with the ark of God on it, and Ahio was walking in front of it. David and the whole house of Israel were celebrating with all their might before the Lord, with songs and with harps, lyres, tambourines, sistrums and cymbals. When they came to the threshing-floor of Nacon, Uzzah reached out and took hold of the ark of God, because the oxen stumbled. The Lord's anger burned against Uzzah because of his irreverent act; therefore God struck him down and he died there beside the ark of God.

Then David was angry because the Lord's wrath had broken out against Uzzah, and to this day that place is called Perez Uzzah.

David was afraid of the Lord that day and said, 'How can the ark of the Lord ever come to me?' He was not willing to take the ark of the Lord to be with him in the City of David. Instead, he took it aside to the house of Obed-Edom the Gittite. The ark of the Lord remained in the house of Obed-Edom the Gittite for three months, and the Lord blessed him and his entire household.

Now King David was told, 'The Lord has blessed the household of Obed-Edom and everything he has, because of the ark of God.' So David went down and brought up the ark of God from the house of Obed-Edom to the City of David with rejoicing.

David the little shepherd boy, the one that was almost overlooked, stood before the prophet of God and the oil of anointing was poured out over his head and his life. As David stood there, destiny lay before him. The prophet probably gazed down on this young lad and thought, 'I nearly missed you, David. I was sure one of your tall, fine, accomplished brothers would be king. I never thought that God would choose a simple shepherd boy like you.' All those of great outward bearing and appearance had been discounted. He was God's choice. Why? Because in David God had found a man with a heart like his own and, Scripture tells us, he would obey him in everything.

The Lord God anointed an amateur, a worshipper, a simple shepherd boy. This man 'after God's own heart' loved the presence of God more than anything else. Later in his life he would pen the words, 'Do not cast me away from your presence or take your Holy Spirit from me' (Psalm 51:11). He who loved God's presence determined that he would bring that presence, the ark of the covenant, back to its rightful place in Jerusalem. Preparations were made and the day arrived. There was celebration, there was singing, there was rejoicing. He threw a party. The presence of the Lord was returning to Jerusalem. As we look at this account, however, we see a change had taken place in the heart of King David.

Once obedient to all God told him to do, he now carried the presence of God, not on the shoulders of the priesthood, but on a new cart. It was probably the best cart David could find – ornate, noticeable, fitting to carry the presence of God. I think it was probably a cart to beat all other carts, but a new cart was not what God wanted when it came to moving his presence from one place to another. It was important for attention to be focused not on the vehicle being used to carry the presence, but on that which was being carried.

Somewhere along the line something had crept into the heart of David. A complacency, a professionalism, a disobedience, perhaps a pride. We need to continually guard our hearts against those things that would seek

17

to creep in and destroy our usefulness in the work of God.

As they proceeded along the way, bringing the presence of the Lord back to its rightful place, we read that the anger of God burned against David. Then the inevitable happened. At the place of trouble and difficulty, Nachon's threshing-floor, that which had begun badly ended disastrously. As the ark was tipped and nearly fell it could not be steadied by the arm of the flesh and a man lay dead beside the presence of God. The party stopped. The instruments fell silent. Everyone backed off. That which was meant to bring blessing and victory was now killing people. David had with him thirty thousand choice men, brave, the best warriors, but at that moment none of them wanted the ark. It was unpredictable, it was messy, it killed people. No-one wanted the presence.

Suddenly, a shuffle was heard in the ghastly silence of the crowd. It wasn't David, nor his choicest men. An unrecognised nobody was coming forward. When no-one wanted the presence, little Obed-Edom said, 'I'll have the ark.' That is exactly what is happening today. Little nobodies are pressing through the throng of somebodies and whilst it might mean the loss of reputation, ridicule or even abandonment they cry, 'I want the presence!'

'But, you might lose your church.'

'Never mind, I want the presence.'

'You may be misunderstood.'

'I only want the presence!'

'This is unpredictable, Uzzah is dead.'

'I still want the presence.'

The Bible tells us that God blessed every area of Obed-Edom's life and then our God of mercy and grace allowed David one more chance of carrying the presence.

This time he did things differently. The ark of God was not carried on a new cart but on the shoulders of the priesthood where it belonged. The presence of God sits best on the shoulders of failed flesh, of mortal human beings – his priesthood. The celebrations commenced, the music began to play, the procession moved forward. This time there was a fundamental difference – something had been addressed in the heart of David.

The robes of kingship had been cast aside, dignity and pride had been abandoned with them. David was an amateur again. The worshipper God first called in the shepherd's field led the presence of God back into Jerusalem, dancing before it with all his might.

However, another professional despised what he was doing. Michal, David's wife, King Saul's daughter, watched the spectacle and despised her husband in her heart. You see, she had been trained in the king's household. She was the king's daughter. She knew how a king should dress, how a king should behave, with dignity and splendour. But God called a shepherd boy, a psalmist, a worshipper, an amateur. He no longer cared for his dignity, he no longer cared for his kingly robes. Abandonment before his heavenly Father was his only desire. God judged Michal because of her attitude and closed up her womb. She thought she knew how a king should behave, but David knew better.

Mark 11:1–10 tells us the story of Jesus's triumphal entry into Jerusalem. The celebration had begun, the people cried, 'Hosanna'. The presence of God was once more being carried into Jerusalem – on a donkey. The problem with many donkeys today is that they think that the crowds are shouting praises to them, and not to the one that they are carrying. Humble servants of the Lord

19

must be willing to be a donkey, so that the glory can go to him. Then they will carry his presence.

The disciples were instructed to go and loose the donkey. That is what the Holy Spirit has been doing in this move, cutting his donkeys free from hurt, pain, anger, bitterness, pride, judgment, division, and then the Father has whispered in thousands of ears,

'David, I have need of you.'

'John, I have need of you.'

'Ken, I have need of you.'

'Lois, I have need of you.'

'Margaret, I have need of you.'

Our hearts have been captured by the love of God time and time again. And now the Lord whispers to us all as he has drawn us to himself, 'I have need of you. Will you carry my presence?'

Chapter 5

Anointed Amateurs

Many times the Lord has spoken to me from the story of David recounted in the last chapter. God loves to cloak amateurs with his presence. Those times when Ken and I have been asked to go and speak at large conferences or in huge churches, we've reminded each other every time that we're only amateurs, nobodies who carry the presence. Even though I could try to dress up in the borrowed armour of another, as they tried to do with David in Saul's armour when he went out to meet Goliath, I cannot. I am only able to throw a few stones, that's all I know. God called me as an amateur and that's all I am. At those times when I can begin to feel puffed up that people may like me, God gives me my amateur status back and I am whole. When God touched our hearts in August 1994 in this new wave of renewal, he changed the heart of a professional pastor, striving and ambitious, reclaiming again the heart of a worshipper that he called when he was a fresh-faced 27–year-old.

The Bible is littered with examples of men, who were great professionals, and when God had dealt with them and given them their amateur credentials they found he then could use them. Moses raised as a prince, behaved as a prince, ruled as a prince, was educated as a prince. According to Acts 7:22–5 he thought the people would recognise immediately that he was the one sent to deliver them.

Moses was educated in all the wisdom of the Egyptians and was powerful in speech and action.
When Moses was forty years old, he decided to visit his fellow Israelites. He saw one of them being mistreated by an Egyptian, so he went to his defence and avenged him by killing the Egyptian. Moses thought that his own people would realise that God was using him to rescue them, but they did not.

Moses supposed his brethren would know Israel would be delivered by his hand, a man learned in all wisdom and knowledge. Yet, when God had put him in the backside of the desert for forty years, when he had been confronted by a bush that burned and was not consumed and that God spoke from, Moses found he had become so amateurish that he pleaded with God to allow another to speak for him. He knew then he was nothing in himself but, clothed in the power of God and his presence, he met God face to face. Such was the glory upon him that his face had to be covered because of the shining radiance.

Moses led Israel right up to the edge of the promised land. He moved in signs and wonders. Those who spoke against him were killed by God because, the word tells us, 'He who touches Moses, touches me.'

Take another example, that of Joseph, a 'professional interpreter' of dreams. Like David and Moses, destiny was written all over his life, yet he began as a proud insensitive young man, clothed in a flamboyant coat,

22

which drew attention to himself and his superiority to his brothers. That coat of pride was later used to deceive his father. That which begins with pride usually ends in deception. The young man whose proud interpreting of dreams angered his brothers had a change of heart during his time of trouble. Sold into slavery, put into prison, forgotten, neglected, he was appointed into Pharoah's court as an amateur. Then God was able to use him, and permitted him to be elevated to be second in command in the whole nation.

When we read of Joseph's encounter face to face with the brothers who had previously betrayed him we see that gone is the pride, gone is the status of the favourite son. His heart had changed. Joseph fell on the necks of his brothers, weeping so loudly everyone could hear. He was God's man, God's amateur. A carrier of his presence.

We in Sunderland were about to be filled with power from heaven and sent into a world of sin as God's amateurs, carriers of his presence.

Chapter 6

How Long Will You Be Offended?

While ministering recently in Brisbane, Australia, I was confronted by a weeping pastor who, challenged by the Lord during the word, responded to the altar call. 'How long will you be offended?' the Lord had whispered to his heart. 'Not one day longer,' was his response.

We in Sunderland were determined to push through all that we may previously have found offensive to find Jesus. In every move of God, the Lord gives us as many reasons to be offended as he does reasons to embrace it. Think for a moment of John the Baptist. All by himself he was a move of God. He didn't build a nice convenient city-centre church, he did just the opposite. Hundreds streamed into the hot Judean desert to him. There, stood in the sweltering heat, they were confronted by the forerunner of the Messiah, and then dipped in a dirty river.

I think if I had been God and wanted a forerunner for my beloved son, John the Baptist would not have been my first choice. I would have chosen a diplomat, a man gifted in public relations, nicely dressed and well spoken. God's choice of forerunner, however, was no diplomat. I'm sure that to many he was an extremely offensive man.

He didn't dress in the normal manner, it was camel's hair for him. Locusts and wild honey were his staple diet and he called the religious 'whitewashed sepulchres' – fine on the outside but with death inside. He offended with his uncompromising message, but still the people kept coming. Why? Because from his mother's womb he had carried the Holy Spirit. He was a carrier of the Lord's presence, and where the presence of God was, people wanted to be. Their lives were for ever changed.

Many Old Testament prophets were very offensive. Lying naked in a field prophesying, for example, takes a lot of beating. Even the Lord Jesus Christ himself was very offensive to the religious. His birth did not fit the religious expectations of his days. Born in a stable in Bethlehem, his birth only announced to a handful of shepherds, causing the wrath of the Pharisees. He healed on the Sabbath in full view of the synagogue. He allowed his disciples to eat with unwashed hands, but worst of all he said, 'Eat my flesh and drink my blood.' Many who were with him were offended and hurriedly left. Jesus, turning to his disciples said, 'Will you also leave me?' Peter, ever the spokesman, said, 'Lord, we have nothing to return to.' They had left their business but more importantly he added, 'You have the words of eternal life.' It is worth noting that Jesus did not run after those who were offended and persuade them to stay. Neither did he explain himself until he was with only those who had chosen to remain despite the offensive words.

Jesus's healing ministry was not at all plain sailing. Sometimes he even spat in people's eyes. 'Ah, but,' you might say, 'it was Jesus's spit.' Nevertheless, it was spit, and he spat in the blind man's eye. Why? To heal him! I can just imagine the outcry if some prominent visiting speaker began to spit on the sick so that they might recover. Yes, Jesus himself was offensive to the religious.

It's almost as if the Lord gives us ample reason to be justifiably offended, fold our arms and legitimately walk away. However, if we are willing to push through the offence, we can find the life-changing presence of God. This truth was vividly emphasised to me a number of years ago. Following the death of our baby son, I was desperately sick and despondent. Surgery to remove a kidney stone had been unsuccessful and my blood pressure was dangerously high. For two years I had been in and out of hospital and we were desperate for God to touch our lives. Ken takes up the story.

Ken's story

'I travelled to Frankfurt because of the encouragement of a friend, Ray Bevan, to a Fire Conference hosted by Reinhard Bonnke. Reinhard had always been a faith hero of mine and, leaving Lois sick at home, I went, hoping this man of God would pray for me and God would do something to meet our desperate need.

'Travelling over to Germany with my heart heavy and eyes clouded with tears, I said, "God, you've got to meet with me this week or I just can't go on under this pressure." That week I spent the whole time trying to be in the place where Reinhard Bonnke could pray for me and impart something that would rescue me and my family from the terrible pit of sickness and despair we had found ourselves in.

'Ray Bevan had told me that after having hands laid on him at the Fire Conference in Harare the year before, he was a changed man. Full of passion and zeal, joy and excitement, he was a human dynamo. I could have done with some zeal and excitement. In fact I needed a dynamo myself, and my wife desperately needed a touch from the hand of God. All week I stood in line for someone to pray for me. Mysteriously I was always avoided. Having been missed in one line, I would join another and be missed again. I listened to my faith hero, Reinhard Bonnke, and rushed to respond to his altar calls. Again no-one came to pray for me.

'However, there was another speaker at that conference. His name was Benny Hinn. I have to confess, I was offended by his ministry. I thought he was too flamboyant, too showy. He kept saying, "Take it." It just wasn't my cup of tea. I noticed his rings and bracelet and made up my mind that I was not going to be prayed for by anyone who sparkled. However, on the last night it was Benny Hinn who was praying for the sick, and suddenly right there he asked for all English pastors to go up onto the platform for prayer.

'I found myself running to the platform. I was too desperate not to respond. There and then I could have made a decision. Either, I could be offended and go home the way I came, or I could push through the offence and see if I could find God in it all.

'"Young man, are you an English pastor?" I heard the evangelist say.

'"Yes," I feebly responded.

'"Come here to me then," he said.

'At that moment I began to walk through what could only be described as liquid anointing about one metre high. I tangibly felt it. All week I had decided how I would receive from God, but I was rapidly finding out God had chosen his own vessel to touch my life. The

27

nearer I got to Benny Hinn the stronger the anointing grew. It felt like electricity pulsating all over my body. I began to shake. The power of God knocked me off my feet as he laid his hands on me. I fell into liquid glory. I bathed in the presence of God. "Pick him up again," I heard him shout, and then he looked me right in the eye and said, "Young man, you will never be the same again."

'I fell to the floor once more in a powerful encounter with my God.

'I got up a changed man. I was filled with a passion for God, and a zeal for his house, and I found I had a great love for the presence of the Holy Spirit. I returned home to England and could have almost flown myself there so excited was I by the fire of God in my heart. My church changed, my ministry had an added dimension, despair gave way to victory. You see, God chose his own vessel. I could have folded my arms, refused prayer and felt justified at walking away. But when I pushed through those things I thought were offensive I found the power of the living God that changed my life for ever.'

Carriers of his presence will not always fit our perceptions. The Lord himself didn't, but the Father asks us to take judgment from our heart, push through any offence that our culture, or tradition, or whatever else places upon us, and we can find God. Carriers of his presence are not always men and women who fit the status quo, who conform to our expectations. Nevertheless they, like those priests who carried the ark on their shoulders, carry his presence to a lost and dying world. First we were to be baptised by fire.

Chapter 7

The Fire Falls

'Fire! Fire!' The great swell of hundreds of voices rose and intruded into our time of prayer and quiet contemplation. It was September 1995 and the final evening of our prophetic conference with Wes Campbell from Kelowna, Canada, was under way. After a wonderfully powerful service, where we had been challenged to burn brightly with the zeal of God, a few of us had returned to the hospitality lounge upstairs.

Norm Strauss, a worship leader also from Canada, remained to lead the nine hundred or more people participating in the ministry time. We fully expected this evening to follow the usual pattern that had emerged over the past year. As people received of the Holy Spirit they most often were overcome by the power of God and lay resting on the floor in the presence of the Lord. Usually there had been a sweet quiet presence of the Father as men and women purified their hearts before him, sometimes accompanied by laughter, weeping or shaking. This evening was quite different!

Extracting myself from the pastors we were praying for, I rushed downstairs to evacuate the building, wondering how the fire could have started. When I reached the bottom of the stairs, an extraordinary sight met my eyes. It seemed to be pandemonium. The whole place was charged with the presence of God.

Unusually everyone was on their feet, arms raised, crying and speaking in tongues, as the Holy Spirit gave them utterance. Spontaneously everyone began to offer praise and worship to the Lord. Intermingled with shouts of 'Hallelujah' and cries of 'Fire!' a Holy Ghost Pentecost was taking place. Reporting later a writer in *Joy* magazine described even the air we breathed as being 'like a tinderbox!!' This was not a fire we were about to put out!

Without prompting, a spontaneous dance began and people filled with the love and the joy of God came together in a conga chain of dance. Bursting open the fire doors, they began to move out from the building and into the streets. Almost one thousand people were dancing around the church building and in the other door.

My mouth dropped open. I was certainly surprised, but the infectious joy and celebration in the place were thrilling. It became obvious that no-one was able to stay in the building. Some ran to the waiting taxi-drivers to tell them about Jesus. Some ran to their hotels and guest-houses to give the message of the gospel to their unsuspecting hosts.

Everyone later described the compulsion to tell anyone they met about their saviour. Without doubt the next day the city of Sunderland knew something extraordinary had occurred. Visitors streamed into the centre. Some came with completed 'Alpha'[1] inquiry forms to enrol for the

1. 'Alpha' is a course devised by Nicky Gumball of Holy Trinity, Brompton, London, for those enquiring into Christianity.

next course. The cellarman of a local hotel had been so impacted by the returning guests that he gave his life to Christ within days. The most dramatic event however was to occur the following evening.

In the three and one half years we had occupied our church building in the East End of Sunderland, our desire had been to impact the local community. However, those who have visited us have been aware of the ongoing car crime and violence in the area. Security guards are employed to protect our property and our persons. Many times we as a congregation had been showered by stones and threatened by local gangs of youths.

On this particular evening they turned out in strength, and asked a co-worker of Wes Campbell who had stayed on with us if they could come in. It was with some consternation we received the telephone call as we rested at home. 'Can we let them in?' Usually these young men and women ran riot – handbags would be stolen and innocent people threatened. But the night before we were sure was a prophetic sign to take what we had received from the Holy Spirit out into the streets. Here were the streets coming to us!

It was with some anxiety we descended that evening to allow the local gangs to come in. They had never wanted to before. So in trepidation we waited to hear reports of the service. Around ten o'clock that evening we were given the news that five of the youths had accepted Christ as their personal saviour and the behaviour of the whole crowd had been impeccable. That began what we believe to be the first-fruits of the harvest in Sunderland.

Every evening these street kids turned up to come and join in our renewal services. It became apparent that the numbers coming could not be contained within the normal pattern of renewal services. We as a church began to pray and reminded ourselves that when God visited us with renewal we embraced fully all that the Father was doing. Now we were seeing the beginning of a harvest that we had longed for and we needed to make room for it. So it was that we decided to give these street kids, so keen to come, exclusive use of our church building on Tuesday and Wednesday evenings.

God had already spoken to me of giving our building to the local community to plant a church while we moved to larger premises. I was learning that God will not be timetabled. He had begun planting the new community church in our building before we were able to move out. He had also drawn to himself a unique man and woman who would most certainly be a bridge into the local community.

Chapter 8

A Captive Now Set Free

As the darkness closed around him, Jim made his way purposefully through the streets of a northeastern housing estate. Late though it was, children still played in the gloom, bottles rolled in the gutter and dogs roamed in packs. Life spewed out in all its urban decay.

'Right, lasses, we're nearly there,' he said to the two young women accompanying him. Wincing, he put his hand to his side where only a few weeks ago he had been stabbed four times. It hurt! He hoped it was healing properly. It was impossible to receive medical attention for these injuries, as the hospitals would only alert the police. 'God, let this inflammation die down,' he prayed, to one he didn't even believe was there.

'Are y'all right, Jim?' asked one of his companions and, bracing himself, Jim spat out his affirmative as they reached their destination. He was nineteen years old and waiting for his 'target' to return – a wealthy foreign businessman, who had neglected to pay his two young companions. Thirty per cent of the debt was owed to Jim.

Silently he drew the baseball bat from his pocket. Here was the hit. 'This'll teach him not to mess with us,' said the same young lady with a gleam of satisfaction on her face. In two strides Jim blocked the way of the startled man. 'I think you owe me some money,' he growled, and the terrified stranger thrust hundreds of pounds into his hands. 'Please don't hurt me,' he whimpered. Twisting his face in a despising sneer, Jim lifted the bat. Minutes later – with the money collected, the victim lying seriously injured in a pool of blood, and with admiring glances from his two companions – Jim felt nothing. Feelings were impossible. It was dangerous in his position to have any emotion.

At that moment Jim had crossed the line from street brawler to the world of organised crime. He had done it! A profitable and 'respected' lifestyle stretched out before him. Days later, propped up on a bar stool, with a comforting pint of brown ale by his side, he gazed around a popular Sunderland night-club. Music was pounding out a primal beat. The heat was stifling, lights flashed on and off revealing daringly exposed female flesh as they writhed and contorted their bodies in front of him.

'How about a dance, pet?' he growled as one particular blonde ventured a little too close. He could see the awe and undiluted admiration in her eyes. His fearsome reputation of violence had awarded him a status with the opposite sex he now exploited.

'What's your name?' he whispered in her ear.

'Linda,' she breathed, and what seemed to be a smirk twisted his features.

'It's so easy,' he thought, as he gave her his undivided attention. Like a spider drawing a fly into a net, he ensnared her emotions. Very soon this young woman, out of devotion to him, would sell her body to many other men to please him, and he would collect another income.

'Life is good,' he whispered with a sigh. He was certain he now had another young woman in his stable. He exploited and yet protected them purely for financial gain.

One evening, standing in the same spot surveying an almost identical scene, Jim's attention was arrested by a stunningly attractive young woman.

'She could earn a fortune,' he whispered to his companion, one of the most feared street fighters in the North of England. As the pair, like cats watching a mouse, surveyed her every move, they became aware of a male presence in attendance.

'Hey, Tracey, who's that?' Jim asked one of the girls who seemed to know everyone. 'That's Elaine,' she said, 'with her husband, Eric.' Jim's eyes narrowed. Elaine could make him huge amounts of money on the game.

That evening, Jim slipped deeper into the alluring mire of sin and reached an all-time low. Eric tearfully gave his consent to his wife selling her body for sex. Intimidating men so that he could use their women initiated a new step towards hell for Jim. Now he had built up a formidable group of girls, supplying clubs, private parties, businessmen, contact magazines with prostitutes. At the same time his violent reputation grew.

Jim now began to spend hours and hours in the gym with a ruthless determination to tone his body to be a perfect fighting machine. Increasing in size to the heavier and heavier weights he was lifting, he became a familiar figure at night-club doors in the city of Sunderland. Wherever there was trouble he sorted it out.

He hungered for power because his gods were control, fear, an elevation in status. As he began to control night-clubs and pubs and give protection, in return he made a large income. Being top dog was vital, and a criminal war was fought until Jim had control.

In the meanwhile he began to enter body-building competitions culminating in the ultimate triumph of British Amateur Body-building Champion of 1987. However, as his girth increased so did his criminal activities, which now expanded to supplying and selling drugs. Eventually he was paid to inflict pain and injury on those who had offended, broken rules or owed money. He has told me since that he broke all of the ten commandments and 'feared neither man nor beast'. He would learn later to fear God!

Hard man though he was, Jim's network of 'friends' in crime became increasingly important to him. He really cared for these men, some more than others. They fought back-to-back, they defended each other. This was a family.

Then trouble struck. One of the owners of a night-club he protected told Jim of a well-known thug who had broken into his home and attacked his family. 'I want you to hurt him for this, Jim,' he yelled in his fury.

It didn't take long. After chasing the man through the centre of the city the next day in broad daylight, Jim caught up with him at a large roundabout. Fury puffed up Jim's features – his face was red, his veins stood out, his neck bulged. Leaping from his car in one move he pulled his hit through the window of his vehicle. Fists pounding, feet kicking, Jim brought a man to the brink of death and was promptly arrested and charged with grievous bodily harm. Sunderland was too 'hot' for Jim and impulsively one evening he fled to Glasgow, a large sprawling Scottish city.

For three years he built up another life of crime in that

city, running prostitutes, dealing drugs. After making a great deal of money, he felt enough time had elapsed for him to return to Sunderland. It was easy to slip back into his old network of crime, living once again with the girl he had abandoned. However, something in his heart disturbed him about the ruthless, violent nature of his occupation.

So a man, who with his criminal activities and physical intimidation had dominated much of Sunderland, was about to meet one stronger and mightier than he had ever known. He was inquisitive and angry to hear of unusual activities taking place in the newly built church, Sunderland Christian Centre, in Hendon. In fact the whole town was talking about what was going on in that previously unheard of church. Some said they had gone mad, laughing and lying prostrate on the floor. Nevertheless, hotels were full and business in town was booming, all because of those flocking to this unlikely centre.

Jim made it his business to discover what was really going on. He watched from a discreet vantage point in the darkness in amazement as, night after night, hundreds of cars pulled up disgorging passengers that had come on a spiritual pilgrimage from all over the world. Security is a nightmare in Sunderland and Jim's eagle eye observed the professional security firm employed by the church protecting visitors and vehicles from the marauding street gangs. 'If you can't beat them, join them!' he thought. If the underworld protected those vehicles not only would they be able to reap financial rewards for their protection, it would open up opportunity for new business.

And yet something about what was going on inside the church got under his skin. He was angry, but couldn't quite place that other emotion. He hadn't felt it for so long. With a sickening realisation he knew he felt fear. For the first time in years, real fear. Why should he feel fear? He intimidated others, so why should some puny hymn-singing fanatics disturb his peace so much?

Jim had not felt any emotion since childhood. Though fathering two children, they were to him more of an inconvenience than a blessing. He really didn't feel love or compassion, ever. To be paid to inflict pain and injury on another human being detaches the emotions from any reality.

The conflict in his heart was about to come closer to home. For the past few years he had lived with his long-time lover, Marie. At the tender age of fifteen, a beautiful young girl, she had been ensnared, abused and exploited by Jim and had become one of his working girls. She was very useful to him and provided a profitable income. Yet, having been raised as a practising Catholic, she hungered for God.

'Marie, I've found Jesus! He's changed my life and I've had a fantastic experience with the Holy Spirit.' It was Sue, Marie's sister. After visiting Sunderland Christian Centre, she had found Christ and been filled with the Holy Spirit. She now experienced the love and peace that had long eluded her. Marie gazed at the radiant face of her sister and a great conflict of emotions tore at her heart. She longed for God as her sister had found him, but still she knew that to find him – especially in that church – would probably mean losing Jim. That she couldn't bear.

However, the Lord was working out his purposes for our city! As we ministered night after night to hungry visitors from all over the world, and basked again and again in the presence of the Lord, we believed God for a harvest of souls. The walls were about to come down between the church and the streets of the world.

Marie decided to visit Sunderland Christian Centre one Friday evening with her sister, Sue. Her life was never to be the same again. The little Catholic girl – embroiled in the organised crime of the city: sin, sex and degradation – found Jesus as her saviour. The Holy Spirit filled her to overflowing. Joy, peace, love and laughter filled her being and she was radiantly transformed. The purity, innocence and beauty of the love of Jesus shone from her face. Though she had always feared losing Jim, she was now prepared to give him up for the saviour who was now her Lord. Night after night she nagged, cajoled, pleaded and begged Jim to come to the renewal services with her.

His fury increased. Not only was the church interfering in his trade, his girlfriend was now involved. He gave in to her pleading, came down to church and sat right in the back. He glanced idly around from his vantage point that night. 'These Christians seem to be having a good time,' he thought. 'This is not what church used to be.' The row of people in front of him began to convulse with laughter, bodies fell from chairs. In spite of himself Jim could not suppress a grin. The whole scene amazed him. Then people at the front began to share what Jesus had done for them.

'Marie,' he hissed. 'These are just sad people. They're needy and have been conned into this stuff, and now you're one of them. You haven't met God. It's rubbish.'

At that moment a woman got up to speak. He slowly regarded her. He did not like her at all. Something about her made him very angry. She was a tall, imposing woman who spoke with a strength he found intimidating. Suzette

Hattingh was the speaker that night. She was far too powerful and confident. Who did she think she was? Had Marie been speaking to her about him? She certainly seemed to know a lot about his life. She could have been speaking to him personally. Little did he realise, God was! As Suzette continued, he grew more and more uncomfortable, yet he didn't know why. Incredulously he realised that again he felt pure fear!

Jumping to his feet, he ran to the door and didn't stop running until he reached the safety of his own front room. Three things shook him. One that he felt anything at all, especially fear. Two, that he ran away. Jim never ran away. Third, and most disconcerting, Marie didn't follow him. Never in all the years she had been with him had she ever disobeyed him before.

Arriving home much later, her face alight with love for the Lord, Jim decided this thing had to be settled once and for all. With a fury he told his partner that next evening he would deal with the pastor and he wanted the matter then forever laid to rest. So, he found himself inside the doors of our church with one purpose in mind, standing at the back of the hall waiting for his opportunity to end this upheaval once and for all. As the call was given that night men and women streamed forward to receive Christ as their saviour. Seizing his opportunity, Jim joined them. Here was a chance to confront Ken. Jim looked at him. Ken was balding, unremarkable. He would certainly pose no threat. I'm so grateful that on that evening the Holy Spirit packed a more powerful punch. Jim approached Ken and looked directly into his eyes. The Lord knocked him flat onto his back. As he lay there at Ken's feet, shocked and confused, struggling vainly to get up, fear gripped him.

Jim's story

'"Get up, get up!" I urged my unresponsive body. As a street fighter, to be on your back on the floor was the most vulnerable place to be. Only a few times in my whole criminal career had I been put on the floor. Now, reluctantly I had to acknowledge God had easily put me there and was keeping me there. Still I struggled. Yet, each limb was pinned to the ground. As I lay, I heard a voice clearly say, "Jim, why don't you give in?" and I immediately found myself saying, "I think I will."

'Immediately a warm blanket of what seemed to be liquid love covered my whole body, a new and unbelievable experience for me began. I began to feel. Emotions vied with each other to surface in my heart. Events, incidents from the past crowded into my mind. Sobbing, for the first time I felt guilt, remorse, repentance, compassion, and yes, even love.

'A love for the one who had proved stronger than me leapt from my previously hardened heart. Tears streamed down my face as I realised Jesus was alive, could forgive me of sin, and best of all, he loved me. Helplessly weeping, something I had been unable to do since I was five years old, I was gently helped to my feet and led to a corner of that church building where I began a personal relationship with Jesus Christ, my saviour.

'Could God ever forgive all of my sins? After all, there was not one commandment I had not broken. The pastor reassured me of the power of the cross of Jesus Christ, and his ability to make me a brand new creature. As I surrendered to God kneeling there on the floor of that church hall, confessed my sins and asked Jesus into my life, an indescribable joy filled my whole body. Returning

41

home that evening I was afraid to sleep in case I shut my eyes and awoke to find the wonderful new feeling had gone. Most of the night I sat up in a chair, but when I eventually gave in to sleep I awoke to find love and joy filled my heart. It still does today.

'I was a different man overnight. I couldn't live the same way, which caused some anxiety to some of my friends in crime. Since I had been personally responsible for so much damage I was committed to winning as many for heaven as I possibly could. Marie and I knew instinctively we should marry if we continued to live together. So with my heart bursting with love for her, I took her as my wife.

'The church at Sunderland Christian Centre took us to their hearts. We experienced love and care like we had never known before. We had a new family. We wanted to serve God with all our hearts. His word became alive to us. Spreading our faith became essential.

'It was with joy I was able to see some of my working girls find Christ and begin to attend church, and the friend who had protected my own life so many times say the same prayer as I had done that memorable evening. Now in our church in Sunderland, unknown to many people, are major criminal figures, worshipping the Lord. My life is for ever changed.'

That evening, as Jim gave his life to the Lord, right there during the ministry time of a regular renewal service, God had chosen a key vessel for the next phase of his move, just as he did with Saul of Tarsus at the beginning of the early church. Jim and Marie matured in the Lord at an extraordinary pace. He was truly one man one minute, another the next. And yet we didn't know the best was yet to come.

Chapter 9

It Took a Miracle

Prior to the visit of Wes Campbell, that memorable evening when we had been deluged with Holy Ghost fire, the Lord had clearly spoken to Ken's heart concerning our church building. Because we had grown so rapidly over the last year the facility we had occupied for less than four years was totally inadequate. Yet how could we leave? We had given so much to build it and it had seemed so vast at the time!

As he thought of the financial implications of taking on another building the Lord clearly told Ken not to sell in order to finance the larger place but to plant a different type of church there, for the local community and the street kids. 'But, Lord,' he had argued, 'no-one from the local community even speaks to us, let alone comes to church. How can you want this?'

'Do it!'

He knew the Lord was serious. I must confess my heart sank. How could we share with our people, who had given everything to build the church, that the Lord had told us to give it away? Many had sold their homes, others had given their life savings.

I needn't have worried! Our people are committed

to following the Father wherever he leads. Though we couldn't see it yet, our hearts said 'yes' to a community church in that building. And now God had brought to himself a man and woman, a human bridge to the local community. 'Between the walls of the church and the streets of the world', the walls were about to come down. Marie's life had also been as profoundly changed as Jim's had been. This is her story.

Marie's story

'Every morning as I attempted to gaze at my reflection in the mirror, I continually found my head turning away. I was no longer looking at me but what I had allowed myself to become and I was terrified. I was scared of me, scared of what I was capable of because I loved Jim so much. My life was sordid. The things I did to please my partner repulsed even me. Nothing could ever describe the wickedness of it all, nor the terror. I wanted Jim but I couldn't bear what he was becoming. He was leaving himself behind and someone else was taking over. Slowly at twenty-five years of age I was turning into an alcoholic. Alcohol could numb the horror of my life. I needed a lot of numbing.

'Then my sister was transformed. Her face radiated with something intangible but something I had longed for. She had found Jesus. She looked new, in fact she was new. I felt as if I had been travelling so long that I had run out of my very life, and in Sue I saw a freshness that gave me hope of a new start.

'"Sue," I said, "I've gone so far down the line, I've got to change even if Jim doesn't. I'm in prison, and now I have a chance to get out." She reached forward and took my hand, and I knew I could not live with my sin any longer.

'"Take me to your church," I cried and fell into her arms. That evening she led me to the place where she had encountered God in such a way as to change the whole course of her life.

'People crowded into the church building which was unlike any I had seen before. The place was packed and there was an atmosphere of excitement. As the service began, some people started to laugh uproariously, others shook, some fell over.

'"That's the Holy Spirit making them do that," Sue whispered in my ear. However, in the midst of all sorts of things I couldn't understand, I knew with a certainty this was where I wanted to be. It was a place where I could be safe, where I could leave my hurt. It was so warm and loving. This is where I could rest.

'That evening as I walked to the front to find Christ, I felt as if someone had picked me up in giant arms. As he held me he whispered into my heart, "This is where we will start", and I could rest and be comforted. The problem of how I could tell Jim swamped me as I returned home. Never in my wildest dreams could I imagine him to experience God as I had done. I could never believe he could feel as I did. I was wrong!

'After fights and tears, nagging and persuading, Jim came to church. As I watched him lying, pinned helplessly to the floor as tears streamed down his cheeks, I witnessed a miracle. Jim became a brand new man and together, we began to read the Bible, pray and talk to many of our friends about Jesus.

'After Wes Campbell's visit to Sunderland, the street kids began to come into church and Jim and I knew

45

we had to get involved. We had found our destiny! Now instead of leading people into hell, we were able to point them to heaven. Night after night the kids came in and we just wanted to be with them. God was moving, and he had taken two people from the gutter and joined us to a family and together we were about to build the kingdom. The street kids have become our mission field. Every evening we turn out to give them more.'

Chapter 10

Don't Cry for Me, Argentina!

July 1995 saw Ken and me exhausted, yet thrilled with all that God was doing. Hundreds still streamed to our church every evening. God had saved extraordinary people, lives were being put back together, marriages were mending, denominational walls had come crashing down. We served the body of Christ together as one. We loved each other, we served each other, we needed one another. It was difficult to imagine then, that God could bring any greater co-operation between us, or take those levels of unity any deeper. We were wrong, and God sent a high-profile Argentinian, one of the key figures in revival there, to confound us even more.

We knew something was going on in Argentina. Certainly John and Carol Arnott had thought it important enough to travel there for an impartation of the Spirit in January 1994, returning to Toronto days before renewal broke out in their church. We had heard Sue Mitchell of the Ichthus fellowship in London speak of the incredible transformation in her husband, Roger, after his visits to Argentina. Our friends Benny and Suzanne Hinn and Suzette Hattingh also told us of their visits and the wonderful move of the Spirit there. Yet I confess, nothing had really grabbed our attention.

So, in July 1995, quite sovereignly, the Lord brought Ed Silvoso to Sunderland. Ed is an international speaker who majors on prayer and the unity of pastors praying together as a key to revival. Since we had an excellent speaker coming into Sunderland, Ken and I thought it a wonderful opportunity to take a much needed holiday. The church would be in very safe hands. We jetted off to Tenerife, sunshine and rest as Ed Silvoso flew into Sunderland. We didn't realise it was the beginning of something new and marked a significant step in our journey into harvest.

The first phone calls home were encouraging. Ed felt the spiritual climate in Sunderland was ripe for revival. It felt like Argentina prior to the ingathering of souls they were experiencing. We were thrilled. Nothing less than revival had been our desire as renewal had broken into our church.

Late one evening, after a day lazing on the beach, the telephone rang. It was Lesley, one of our secretaries.

'Guess what Ed Silvoso prophesied tonight,' she said. 'The Lord is about to take down the fence that surrounds our church property because the local community is about to come in and it will no longer be necessary!'

'Oh, thank you, Lord! Thank you, Lord!' Ken cried. 'I so needed confirmation I was hearing your voice.' With no natural indication to confirm what he had felt, it was scary to ask your church to give up their building for which they had sacrificed so much, for a community that were hostile in the extreme. Up to that point he had shared the vision only in confidence with his closest leaders, so Ed's words brought joy and peace to his heart. Whatever else

48

was relayed from Sunderland over the next few days we were ready to listen to.

The next unusual thing to occur was the reaction of my father, Herbert. A man never given over to emotion displays or sudden whims he was adamant in his love for this man Ed Silvoso. A Holy Spirit connection was put in his heart and at seventy-four years of age he was determined to visit Argentina and see first-hand that about which he was hearing.

In all the years Herbert has sat in our church he has always advised and never imposed either his thoughts or his will, but he was coming very close to it now.

'This is the way forward, Ken,' he excitedly persevered on the hotline to Tenerife. My questioning heart was open, but I was not persuaded. Things were marvellous as they were. Pastors and leaders were united, God was refreshing us, and blessing our church. Neither Ken nor I had yet grasped the significance of Ed's words as he talked of taking cities for Jesus by united pastoral prayer. Yet the seeds had been sown. We always think God wants to bless our individual churches. No. He wants to take our cities.

The other major direction Ed Silvoso brought to us was that of prayer houses where church people committed themselves to pray daily for their neighbours, thus family by family winning their streets and communities. He encouraged our people by recounting salvation after salvation accomplished this way in Argentina. We returned from Tenerife to be presented with a list of 150 prayer homes in our church committed to pray in a new and determined way for their neighbours. Little did we realise the incredible and tangible fruit that this would bring, beginning with one of our secretaries, Denise, not long saved, and her family life recently transformed during renewal.

Slowly we were mounting a new wave which was about to sweep through our church. It began with Denise's story.

Chapter 11

From Tragedy to Triumph

As Denise prepared the lunch whilst at the same time
trying to unpack the shopping bags, her practised eye
as a mother glanced into the lounge. Her three-year-old
daughter kept herself busy stacking up her favourite toys
and her baby gurgled happily in the crib. A familiar scene.
Today, however, she felt an unusual disquiet and hesitantly
reached out yet again to telephone her parents. She felt a
growing need for them to do something decisive. What it
was, though, she couldn't imagine.

As her eyes were drawn again to the children – a picture
of domesticity, so cosy, so reassuring – she did not feel
the calm which normally would accompany such a scene.
Surely nothing could be seriously wrong? Until one week
ago everything in her life and that of her family had been
wonderful. She pondered over what had changed in so
short a time. She had a happy and fulfilling marriage,
healthy children, and Glenn had begun a new job that
week, after receiving promotion. It wouldn't be long before
the house in Leeds would be sold and the family would all
be together again.

Yet, as Denise replaced the telephone receiver having
been reassured by her parents once again, she knew in her

51

heart that something was seriously wrong. Her much-loved husband of four years, an out-going go-getting extrovert, had worked one week in his new job. It had seemed to be a wonderful opportunity for the whole family, a well-earned promotion, a chance to escape from West Yorkshire and a promising future for their children. Strangely, as the week which began with such promise progressed, it began to change into a nightmare.

With every call home, her husband's confidence seemed more shattered. His belief in himself disappeared fast. She consoled herself with the thought that once home, surrounded by his family, his old confidence would return. After all, nothing like this had ever happened before.

Now, however, it was Saturday morning; her husband was home, and things definitely seemed worse. For the first time Denise was witnessing her husband openly weeping in despair.

'I've failed,' he sobbed. 'I've let down my family, I'm no good.' By the minute he grew more and more disturbed. He had suddenly become a complete stranger – one moment pitiful, the next raging.

Alarmed by her husband's mounting agitation, Denise impulsively did something she had never done before. Pouring out a large neat whisky, she thrust it into his shaking hand. Perhaps the alcohol would settle his nerves, and everything could return to normal. Unfortunately, far from calming her husband, the whisky increased his agitation and, as his voice rose and his weeping grew more unrestrained, a panic gripped her heart.

'I'm no good to you or the children,' he yelled. Denise began to weep and plead with her husband to come with her and talk to someone who could help with whatever troubled him. 'No!' he screamed, and his refusal was signalled by the fact that within minutes he had consumed a large proportion of the bottle of whisky sitting on the table in front of him.

Because of the fear rising within her, Denise began to argue with her husband, and demand that he stop drinking the spirits. Without warning Glenn jumped up in a haze of alcohol and tears, then ran out of the house clashing the door behind him.

Sensing the atmosphere, the baby began to cry and the toddler screamed out in fear. Denise gathered one child under each arm and rushed to the door to follow him. As she tugged wildly at the handle, the realisation slowly dawned. Her husband had locked the door behind him. At that moment a car roared into life and the tyres screeched as it was driven off at high speed. Frantically sitting the sobbing children on the floor, she scrambled to the back door, stumbling in her distress, knowing it was imperative that someone stop her drunken angry husband from driving the car. Desperation consumed her.

'Help!' she cried. Denise was locked in her home with her children screaming in terror as she beat upon the windows.

It seemed like an eternity had passed when a police car drew up outside the house and a policeman held up a bunch of keys as he walked towards her. Relief swept over her in waves as she recognised her husband's keys. Obviously he had been arrested for drunk driving.

'Thank God you've come,' she sighed as he opened the door with the keys. Calmly and compassionately he conveyed news that was to shatter her world.

'I'm afraid your husband has been involved in an accident,' he began. Her beloved husband, after driving out of the street, had driven straight into a brick wall nearby, and had been killed instantly. Denise felt deep sobs rack her body. This could not be happening. How could it have come to this? She ran to the privacy of the bathroom and locked the door. She needed to shut out the world.

'Denise, Denise.' She became aware of a familiar voice calling out her name and, opening the door, fell into the comforting arms of her mother. Looking around her home through swollen red-rimmed eyes, she knew in that moment her life had changed forever. The policeman was now joined by a sergeant.

'I'm sorry,' he said. 'I'm afraid we need you to come with us.' Within minutes she was in the rear of a police car.

With her father's strong and comforting arms clasped around her, Denise was stunned into silence by the unreality of it all. Only two hours ago she had been routinely peeling the potatoes for lunch. Now she was walking into a cold and forbidding morgue.

'Is this your husband?' the policeman gently asked, and as Denise gazed down into the gaping head wound crudely packed with gauze, the bruised distorted features and the unnatural stillness, hot tears began to course down her cheeks. A profound sense of grief began to take hold of her as she realised the impossible had happened; her husband was dead. Lost and alone, within a morning her world had fallen apart.

'Yes,' she gasped. 'It's him.'

The next few days passed in a whirl, though Denise spent most of her time draped over her husband's coffin in the chapel of rest.

'Come on, Denise, you need your rest,' her mother would say as she dragged her away from the forbidding room. She was tormented every waking moment by the fact that she had given her husband alcohol to drink, and her last words to him were not what she would have wanted. Could she have done or said anything to save him?

What could have gone wrong? There was no explanation for the events that had unfolded that week. Glenn, the man who had stood by her side for many years, had in one week become a stranger, and here she was left alone with two young children, guilty, grieving and traumatised.

'Oh Dad, how am I going to cope?' she asked again and again. Immediately, in secret, began a pattern that would prove more than destructive in the days and years that lay ahead. In order to sleep, in order to cope, in order to live, Denise turned to the bottle. No-one else knew, but day by day, week by week, her dependence on alcohol grew until sleep never came until at least one litre of wine had been consumed.

Of course, this affected her children. They were too young to know what substance altered their mother's moods, but suddenly being without a father, and having a mother who wept in grief or slept over-long they too were deeply traumatised. Denise remembers her three-year-old daughter, Natalie, becoming a mother to her, while she herself became the child. The three-year-old mother's head resting on her knees comforted her parent, whilst the overburdening of responsibility being placed upon her young shoulders was storing up to explode at a later date. So, as Denise's dependency on alcohol grew and Natalie's sense of responsibility and fear increased, they stumbled on.

Three years later, Denise's family were becoming

increasingly concerned. Not knowing of her drink problem, her anxiety, depression and despair unnerved them. It was with relief they persuaded her and the girls to join her mother on a holiday to Spain. For the first time, she began to unwind, despite becoming irritated by her mother and fellow guests as they tried to manoeuvre her towards a widower, with three young children, holidaying in the same hotel.

Richard had lost his beloved wife to cancer only one year previously. He too was lost and alone, and one evening whilst dining together under the stars Richard and Denise decided they liked each other, also perhaps more importantly their children liked each other too. Richard lived in Sunderland and Denise visited him regularly after returning from Spain. Both lonely, both needy, both lost, they fell in love and brought their families together. Denise, Natalie and Kimberley moved to Sunderland to join Richard, Marisa, Victoria and Christopher. Naturally, they expected a happy ending but their individual problems still remained and the pressure of bringing two families together brought them to breaking-point. Denise, who was still drinking heavily, decided she had made a mistake. She had acted prematurely. The marriage was over.

This was the point at which Ken and I met them. A close family member asked if we could counsel them, and it was our joy to lead them to Jesus Christ who became their personal saviour. They had found hope. The whole family became an integral part of Sunderland Christian Centre and Denise and Richard grew in leaps and bounds. They became key members, their marriage cemented and Denise was miraculously delivered from alcohol dependency.

However, the family had not really become a united

family. The problems remained and the children all had difficulties of their own because of the traumas they had endured. Natalie in particular who had suffered so much was showing increasingly disturbing behaviour as she grew towards adolescence. Richard and Denise had found the Lord but knew they were still grieving for their partners. The family needed deep healing and much help. Professionals suggested psychiatric help for Natalie. We all thought much counselling, love and support lay ahead. The family lived on in an emotional limbo, and problems with the children increased, particularly with Kimberley, Natalie and Christopher.

Natalie could not bear to let her mother out of her sight. She was repeatedly sent home from school, since her distress could not be settled and she would weep with abandon until she saw her mother again. A school phobia resulted. At twelve years of age, playing away from home with friends, going out to tea, sleeping at someone else's home, going to school, or attending church youth group were all an impossibility. The trauma of her past had left deep scars. She had periods of uncontrollable weeping and depression and school posed insurmountable problems.

To add to the distress and turmoil, Kimberley, Denise's youngest daughter, suffered horrifying night terrors, screaming uncontrollably most nights; and Christopher, Richard's youngest, was ungovernable at home and school.

Natalie had transferred to senior school and the head of house and her form teacher were more than seriously concerned by her fear, tears and lack of communication at school. All concerned felt the school psychological services were needed, and perhaps family guidance. Denise explained fully to the head of house the trauma

57

of Natalie's background and asked that since the family were committed Christians they would like to pray for their daughter before handing her over to the psychologists.

The family needed help. They got it. On the Sunday in August 1994 when the power of the Holy Spirit swept through Sunderland Christian Centre for the first time, it was the children who were the first to be impacted by the power of God. That morning Natalie, Kimberley and Christopher lay on the floor in the presence of the Lord for over two hours. I remember looking on the tiny form of Christopher, his face so sweetly upturned towards the Lord, angelic almost, and knew with a certainty the impossibility of a child so young lying prostrate without movement for so long a time in the ordinary way. Richard and Denise waited patiently, weeping as they sat on the floor alongside their children, and when finally they did emerge from the presence of the Father, gathered them into their arms. Natalie, Kimberley and Christopher were never the same again.

Kimberley slept sweetly through the long dark hours every night. Christopher began to co-operate calmly both at home and at school, and Natalie was a different person. Each day for Denise was a revelation. When Natalie went home she realised to her dismay she had a slight 'jerk' and immediately wondered how she could explain it to her friends. However, that evening she felt the Lord had said to her, 'You only jerk because from time to time I give you a little touch from my hand, to remind you that I am always with you. You are never alone.' Immediately her fear of separation from her mother was over. School in September was no longer a problem. Her confidence grew and she matured in leaps and bounds.

Three months later the school tutor wrote to her parents,

'Natalie has grown in confidence at an almost unbelievable rate. She now relates well to her peers and is improving all the time in her contact with adults.' Her head of house reported: 'Dear Mrs Wilson, I am so very impressed with Natalie's attitude to school – what a change. No longer do we need the help of the Educational Psychologist Services as Natalie has increased dramatically in confidence.'

Denise had experienced first-hand the power of God. She could believe for anything, and when challenged one year later by Ed Silvoso for her home to become a prayer house for her neighbours and her street she readily responded. Number 12, Belle Vue Road, Ashbrooke, Sunderland, was dedicated as a house of prayer. God had given her and her family a reason for living. As they had laughed, jerked, been shaken and wept, they knew they were being filled to overflowing with the power of the Holy Spirit. How much so however, they had yet to discover.

Chapter 12

The Power of Prayer

Every Thursday morning Denise and the little group of ladies in her prayer house began to stretch out their hands across the road and pray for a very needy neighbour. As soon as she moved into the street Denise was aware that the lady over the road had a very serious problem. She watched unobtrusively as a young woman of about thirty years of age was lifted in and out of the house and into a car. She shook uncontrollably. There was no life in her limbs. She appeared to be just like a rag doll. Denise thought she had Parkinson's disease and, filled with compassion, the ladies of the prayer house stretched out their hands towards Elaine's house and prayed fervently. None of them were anyone who would seem in any way special, but all were in unity, all filled with the power of God.

Denise began to inquire of her neighbours what the problem was with such a young woman, the mother of three young children, and learned she had recently suffered a serious accident. At three months pregnant, Elaine had woken in the middle of the night, got up to use the bathroom, had become faint and fallen down the stairs from top to bottom. The result was a brain injury. Not able to wash, clothe, feed or care for herself, her sister had moved in to take care of the whole family. Elaine was in despair. Here is her story.

Elaine's story

'For months I sat in my hospital bed, unable to speak, eat or do anything for myself. I was aware only of tears, flowing unchecked down my face many hours of the day. I longed to communicate, I longed to hold my children, I longed to live again, and each day I sank deeper and deeper into a well of despair. The doctors told me I had injured the back of my brain and really no-one could predict how my condition would develop or even if it would ever improve at all.

'The only thing the doctors were certain about was that it would be advisable to have my pregnancy terminated. Having been raised a Catholic, that decision I found impossible and yet the future offered me no hope. Months later there was no improvement and I was allowed to go home into the care of my devoted sister, a nurse from the major hospital in our area. She took care of all of my most basic needs, and those of my husband and children. For me life was not worth living, I had lost myself.

'I did know that the family over the road were church-going people – everyone in the street knew that – but I had never talked to them, because they moved in shortly after my accident. I have always been a practical, down-to-earth person, never given over to fancies, feet firmly on the ground, and yet the most unusual thing began to happen.

'Every Thursday morning I was aware of waves of warmth and love coming from Denise's house across the road, to flood over me and my home. Truly I was totally astounded by what I felt but I couldn't deny it. I knew I was feeling waves of something wonderful coming across the road. I knew without doubt they were praying for me. Each week I waited in excited anticipation for the waves of power and love to flow over me, and each week I got stronger.

'Eventually, I was totally restored to health, and my baby was born healthy and normal. With tears streaming down my face I hesitantly made the journey across the road to thank Denise for praying for me. I was nervous. What if it was all in my mind? What if they had never been praying at all? Yet I knew I had to go and thank her.

'I knocked and as the little figure opened the door and looked questioningly at me I began to weep. "Thank you for praying for me," I blurted out. "I felt the waves of love coming across the street." Then I had to laugh at the astonishment that crossed her face. "You knew we were praying?" she gasped. "Yes," I said. "I felt it." As we wept together that night Denise told me of the love of Jesus Christ who had died on the cross for me. Raised a Catholic I had a religion but I didn't have a saviour. I gave him my life and found a reason for living. He means everything to me.

'Soon I was attending Sunderland Christian Centre where the people did all manner of unusual things. They laughed, fell on the floor, cried as the Holy Spirit came on them. This same Spirit drew me to Jesus. I too was filled with the Spirit and a new dimension was added to my life. My sister who had moved in to care for me, because of my healing, accepted Jesus as her saviour, as did my friend. We are on fire for God and want to see our city won for him. Now my home is a prayer house and we are stretching out our hands to pray for another neighbour. Watch out!'

*   *   *

As in the case of Jim and Marie Richardson, God had miraculously intervened into the lives of key people and drawn them to himself. Elaine and Linda were about to be used in one of the ministries which is seeing miraculous salvations. We cannot keep up with the river of humanity coming to Jesus through their enterprise in our church: a drop-in centre for the needy. It is not just social action they are involved in, the power of God permeates everything they do. Desperate people are being clothed, fed, cared for and are finding Christ, their lives utterly transformed.

I am reminded again of the Salvation Army, propelled into social action by the power of the Holy Spirit. 'Go for the lost and go for the worst,' the great general had said. That we now were doing, spearheaded by Elaine and Linda, miraculously saved in one of Ed Silvoso's prayer houses. More was yet to come.

Chapter 13

Land of the Eagles

Immediately following Ed Silvoso's visit to us here in Sunderland, where I am certain he deposited some of that revival spirit, one of our ministry teams prepared to leave for Albania, Land of the Eagles. We were about to see a new wave begin to flow with our ministry teams as they went out. A young pastor, Paulin Valajeti, and his wife, Luli, had struggled on there, with an Anglican priest called Dudley Powell, attempting to build a church and meet the needs of their local community. Growth had not been a fruit of their church. They were sixty needy people somewhat discouraged and needing a visitation. Paulin had been saved some five years previously, at the peak of Communist dictatorship.

Albania was bleak, dispirited, oppressed, disheartened and poor. Everywhere there were eyes watching, informers ready to give you over to the authorities. Even to complain of lack of tomatoes in the shops could result in a prison sentence. Paulin lived with his extended family of fourteen members in just two dingy rooms.

Everywhere everyone looked over their shoulders, resentful yet afraid. One day Paulin noticed someone new in the local coffee house. An Englishman was talking about Jesus. Forbidden to speak to foreigners, Paulin hovered from a distance and then plucking up courage sat down to talk. Even there eyes were watching, and someone informed. He was hauled away and imprisoned immediately.

Surrounded by dank stinking walls, in darkness, thigh-deep in freezing water, Paulin was imprisoned. Not for one moment could he allow himself to fall asleep or even stand still for too long. If he slept he fell into the freezing waters. If he remained still he was in danger of quietly dying of hypothermia. He lifted his heart to the Jesus he had only just heard about and determined, once free, he would find out more.

The moment he was released Paulin went searching for the Englishman who had told him about God, and found him in a city about twenty miles away. There he gave his life to Jesus, whatever the risks, and God's man was called to the ministry The underground church met in homes, in forests, in fields, wherever they could and Paulin was arrested and beaten for Jesus from time to time. On a train one day he met the young Muslim girl, Luli, who was to become his wife and she too joined the large numbers of Paulin's family in the two rooms in Berat, Albania. A torn, tattered curtain stretching across the corner of the room afforded them their only privacy.

Encouraged by an Anglican priest, Dudley Powell, Paulin joined the ministry. His sixty-strong church was awaiting a visit from a ministry team from the notorious Sunderland Christian Centre. Paulin didn't really know what to think. It had been a very bad year for Luli, his wife. She had lost both her brothers, one with cancer – unable to be treated even for pain due to the lack of drugs in Albania – another electrocuted in the shower. They were desperate.

Meanwhile, back in Sunderland, the team prepared for departure. Ordinary pew-filling people with an extraordinary God. Caroline led the team – this is her story.

Caroline's story

'It had all begun two months before when Dudley and Jenny Powell, sponsored by Aid to the Nations had come to the Randy Clark conference. They had come rather warily, having read negative reports of the Toronto Blessing in various evangelical magazines.

'However, Dudley spent most of the conference on his face and returned home to the two churches in Berat and Kuchove for which he has oversight, convinced that what was happening was of the Lord. The immediate effect was a dramatic increase in conversions which has since continued. Knowing that they were shortly coming back to England for a holiday, Dudley and Jenny decided not to mention the rather peculiar manifestations they had seen in Sunderland.

'As they arrived back in England a team of six from Sunderland landed in Albania. This visit had been arranged many months before as a two-week evangelistic mission with the church in Kuchove. We'd spent the last year "marinated" in the phrase "the nameless and faceless move of God" and we were about to learn what that really meant. We spent the first week doing outreach evangelism with the church. But we felt that God wanted to do something more so we prayed for direction.

'As I rested one afternoon I heard the noise of the wind moving through the trees, and then torrential rain fell. As I watched I was reminded of prophecies which had been given that where the floods came, there God's blessing

66

would flow. The Albanian pastor, Paulin, came to visit in the evening and reported that in the nearby town of Berat they were wading up to their knees in water! But what made us really take note was that Paulin said he had never known it rain like that at that time of year. We took this as our direction and asked Paulin if we could pray for the outreach team.

'The six of us began to pray – we were just ordinary people, not one "big name" amongst us – but the river which had flowed through us all year was now being imparted to some very hungry Albanian young people. We had made it a deliberate policy not to mention any of the manifestations we'd seen in Sunderland – we wanted there to be no element of manipulation, suggestion or hype!

'But suddenly, to our amazement, most of those being prayed for fell to the floor and began to tremble, jerk and laugh. Then one young man started to shout, "Jesus, save me! Jesus, save me!" Later he stood up, grabbed a guitar and leapt around the room praising the Lord. He testified that as he lay on the floor he had felt a black cloud leave him. Many others were deeply affected at this time, with long standing problems being resolved and many coming to know Jesus for the first time.

'That marked the beginning of an amazing move of the Holy Spirit which continues to this time. For nearly six months in Berat and Kuchove there have been conversions each week and sometimes every day. However, soon after the team's return it was clear this had been no ordinary trip. As we had begun to see a stream of salvations in Sunderland, we were about to hear of a veritable flood in Albania. Revival had come to Kuchove.'

Dudley's story

'We came in May to the Randy Clark conference in Sunderland from Albania, desperately dry and in need of spiritual refreshing. We weren't at all convinced that this was for us. Having read various negative reports in the Christian press about the Toronto Blessing, we had serious question marks about things we had heard and certain things we needed reassurance about.

'On the first day, all the things we needed reassurance about were given. There was a strong emphasis on sin and repentance, on the centrality of the word of God, and teaching that any move of the Spirit needed to be rooted in the Scriptures. We were encouraged by the attitude of the leadership, and their very mature and positive approach to what was happening.

'By the afternoon of the second day every apprehension we had was laid to rest. The Lord really ministered to both myself and my wife. I spent an awful lot of time on the carpet – there was one session where for the entire sermon I was flat on my face. One evening, when Ken Gott wanted to pray for all the overseas leaders and we were in the central aisle, as soon as people started praying I fell down on the ground and I was down there quite a long while. After a while I had a tremendous sense of the Lord's presence and peace. Then I thought it was time to get up, but I had great difficulty doing that – I was staggering like a drunk. A lady came by with a dustbin – she was tidying up at the end of the meeting. She put the dustbin down behind me and came to help me. The end of it was that I ended up firmly embedded in the dustbin – to much hilarity from those around me.

'The important thing was the reality of the Lord's

presence. The manifestations aren't the important thing. What is important is the reality of him in our lives. We were much encouraged by the conference and went back with a renewed relationship with the Lord and a renewed desire to dig deeper into God's word and to see the Lord at work. That is what has happened. We have seen many conversions, we've seen people dramatically changed, we've seen the Lord ministering to Christians and sorting out problems and taking away hurts from the past and some miraculous healings. We've also seen the demon-possessed released – it's just like it was in the days of Jesus and in the Acts of the Apostles.

'The most amazing thing, though, in the country of Albania, which is a very hard country in which to work, is that we've seen amazing conversions with testimonies which would honour many books. We could write a whole book with testimonies of believers we work with. It has been most encouraging to us. Here are the stories of a few of the converts.

'**Arifi** was converted in the summer when the team from the Sunderland Christian Centre was in Kuchove. He's a young man who was a hoodlum. Most people in Kuchove were frightened of him because he had a shocking reputation. He used to sell drugs in Greece, and on one occasion he actually shot and wounded someone. But now he's given his life to the Lord and he has a gift of evangelism and has brought many of his friends to the fellowship and witnessed to many people. He's a great blessing because when we get the criminal element in they respond to him and we don't have to worry about them!

'**Juli** was converted just a few weeks ago. He was standing at the door during a Sunday service. The appeal came and he went rushing forward. Juli was a satanist, dressed in black from head to foot. Around his neck was a cross with a skull on it – a symbol of satanism. Before he prayed the prayer of repentance he took off the cross with the skull, and as we prayed it was obvious that the Lord was at work in a very deep way. You could tell that his prayer really came from his heart. He gave his heart to the Lord.

'**Sokol** described himself as a criminal. He didn't give his life to the Lord in the meeting but Paulin was talking to him on the street when he said he couldn't possibly accept the Christian faith because he planned to kill three people during that day and he was also planning a couple of robberies. Paulin said, "That's the very reason why you need to accept Christ and that's the reason that Christ had died on the cross for you." He gave his life to the Lord. That was on the Tuesday, and on the Friday he came to the breaking of bread meeting and was about to take communion. Paulin said to him, "Don't you think that's a bit soon?" He said, "No. Christ has washed my sins away and I'm forgiven." So he took communion.

'That night he had a vision, in which he was standing before Christ. He knelt down. On his left and right he was surrounded by all his friends who wouldn't kneel down. He kept on imploring them to kneel because Christ was holy – but they wouldn't. Jesus approached him and took him by the arm and said, "Don't worry about your friends. You're coming with me." And as Jesus started leading him to heaven he woke up to discover it was only a dream – but for a young believer this was a tremendous encouragement and reassurance that he was on the right path.

'**Beti** – a young Christian aged nineteen – is very committed and the Lord has done a good work in him. All his friends are young hooligans and it is his own testimony

70

that he was once the same. He's been very faithful, but his story illustrates the temptations which believers face. He's got a friend in Italy working as a pimp who spoke to Beti on the phone one day and told Beti to get himself a girl and bring her to Italy and he would make good money. This was a great temptation to him. Without any difficulty he found a girl who was willing to go and work in Italy as a prostitute. Then he asked for prayer just saying that he had a problem and a temptation – he didn't say what it was. But subsequently when he spoke to his friend on the phone he said, "I'm not coming." His friend said, "You're a fool," but Beti said, "To you I may be a fool but before the Lord I'm honourable." He's a qualified plumber and we've since been able to supply him with the tools he needs to set up a business so that he can get honest employment. This is a real problem for Albanians. There are plenty of Albanians with abilities to do things but they haven't the actual opportunities to do the work because they haven't the tools and equipment. To keep believers in Albania by helping them to find employment is a priority to us.

'Sabriu is a 22–year-old young man. Before he became a Christian he was a drunk and a fanatical Moslem. He had contact with some of the believers. He was a man who drank because his life was empty. One of the believers said to him, "If you're a Moslem, why don't you believe what the Koran says? In the Koran it says that Jesus came to earth, that he died and that he rose again. If that's in the Koran why don't you believe it?" He went home and looked up the appropriate passage. When he saw that it referred to Jesus he closed his Koran and opened the Bible. Subsequently he gave his life to the Lord. Sabriu no longer drinks – he's a very committed Christian. He's been to the YWAM (Youth With a Mission) discipleship training course and now works full-time in the fellowship up in the castle area of Berat. We've seen his life transformed. We would describe him as a trophy of grace.'

Within three months of the team visiting Kuchove, the church had increased from sixty to 350 as 290 people found Christ as their saviour. At the time of writing another ministry team is preparing to go within the month to Albania, to baptise all these new converts. The salvations are still flooding in – sixteen last week alone.

And God was about to do the same for us in Sunderland.

Chapter 14

Revival in Your Back Pocket

The visiting speaker, well-known for her accurate prophetic ministry, was visiting Sunderland Christian Centre
for the first time. 'Stand up, lady,' she said to Mary, my
mother, not knowing who she was. 'Tell the man of God,'
she began, 'I am about to take him out to a new place
and he will return with revival in his back pocket.' Mary
began to cry. Only one week previously we in the church
had taken up an offering to send both her and Herbert
my father to Argentina to witness first-hand the revival
going on there. We believed they would come back to us
with something for Sunderland.

'Three times the devil has tried to snuff out his life,'
she went on, 'but God has spared him to see revival!' My
mother and I were puzzled. Herbert had experienced two
brushes with death through cancer, but the third attempt
at his life eluded us.

That evening we rushed home, full of excitement, God
had spoken. Unfortunately difficult circumstances met
us. Herbert, who had been in an eldership meeting
with Ken, had a sudden and total amnesia. He was
confused, disorientated, and could not remember at
least the last forty-five minutes of the meeting. Every

sentence he uttered was forgotten almost as soon as the words came from his mouth. He unknowingly repeated himself continuously.

Concerned at what might be happening to my Dad, I telephoned the duty doctor. 'Since your father is seventy-four,' he advised, 'take him straight down to the hospital casualty department.' We began to pray as Mary and Herbert left for the hospital. About three in the morning Mary telephoned to say the doctors were sure Herbert had suffered a transitory ischaemic attack, often a prelude to a full-blown stroke. Suddenly we were reminded of the prophet's words that evening. Once more the devil had tried to take Herbert's life – even at the same time as the prophet was speaking – and he was spared. Within days he was on his feet and raring to go.

It was then with a little anxiety that we waved him off for Argentina five days later – a man determined nothing would stop his quest for revival, and didn't the prophet of God say he would bring it back in his 'back pocket'? – whatever that was to mean.

From the day he met Jesus at fifteen years of age Herbert had pursued only one passion – winning souls for Jesus. He was born in Manchester in 1922 to a young unmarried woman who, unable to keep her baby because of the stigma of illegitimacy in those days, paid others to care for him. With no adequate system of social services, no-one to watch over the welfare of such children, abuse, neglect and emotional starvation were commonplace. Herbert's mother paid anyone and everyone who could take care of her son to do so. Many things relating to those days he has never spoken of. Those things that he could describe, reflect the shocking hardships that were the norm then.

As a three-year-old he can remember being abandoned

for hours to sit on an old sewing-machine throughout a thunderstorm, totally unattended and in total darkness. Too small to get down from the table, he sat in terror as lightning flashed and thunder roared, with no mother to comfort him, no father to reassure. He was taken in by a couple who had other such children in their care. Their surname was 'Wood' and he took their name. Herbert Wood was now living in Portwood, Stockport in a very poor home but with a little more stability.

The lady of the house was a distant, unloving woman, but the man that he now called 'father' loved Herbert. Holding himself like a sergeant-major, he instilled bearing, pride and discipline into the little rejected scrap of humanity placed in his keeping. Herbert liked it there. He had a paper round. Sometimes he went to school. Although only eight years old, he was a smoker and he lived in the streets, kicking a ball often until long past the fall of darkness.

Often with his jumper embarrassingly held together with safety pins, feet unshod, he would find himself gazing into the lighted rooms at Christmas-time where some of his friends, his 'betters', were invited to parties. With his nose pressed longingly against the glass pane, his heart tore against the injustice of it all. Hot tears coursed uninvited down his cold cheeks. There was Tommy and Fred but he, Herbert, illegitimate and poor, was excluded. He wasn't good enough! Wonderfully, in the near future he would be good enough for God's family and would find an acceptance in Christ that no-one could deny.

When he was nine years old, a lady, who came to give him sweets every Wednesday, knocked purposefully on the door where he lived. 'Right, Herbert,' she said. 'You never knew it, but I'm your mother and I'm taking you away with me now. Gather your things.' Herbert felt sick. The bottom had dropped out of his world. The home in which he had found some stability was to be wrenched from him. The man he called 'father' was to be so no longer. A stranger calling herself his mother was about to take him away. His bravado crumpled and he gave way to tears.

At bedtime, when he could no longer mask the despair, the tears flowed as he sobbed into his pillow, longing for the man he called 'father'. Forbidden to see him, their only contact was during school hours, when 'father' would turn up with hot pies to make sure Herbert was properly nourished. He was a man who truly cared.

Herbert was now forced to take another name and he became Herbert Harrison, and at a young and tender age he took on responsibility for the troubled woman who was his mother. Life had dealt very hard with her. Struggling, she had worked night and day to keep her two children from orphanages. Insecure and despairing, Herbert would occasionally return home to find his mother suicidal – once his arrival was just in time. The responsibility for both his mother and his sister weighed heavy on his young shoulders.

One day an old gypsy woman, shopping on the streets of Portwood in Manchester, handed out a gospel tract to a harassed young woman. Pushing it to the bottom of her bag she thought no more about it until, unpacking her shopping later, she uncurled it and began to read. That's how Herbert's mother learned about Jesus. With tears streaming down her face she prayed the prayer of repentance and asked the Lord Jesus Christ to make her a brand new person. For a few days Herbert knew something was different with his mother. Instead of depression there was joy. Instead of threats of suicide she was singing. Instead of pleading with him not to leave her alone she was always at church. In fact she was a brand-new woman.

Inevitably she wanted her family to experience the love and joy of Jesus that had so radically changed her life. A compulsive card player and gambler, an angry young man, Herbert didn't want to know her saviour. One evening her persuading produced results. Sitting beside her in church he heard for the first time about the second coming of the Lord Jesus Christ. Although he didn't understand this it did have a profound effect. Some nights later Herbert gave his life to Christ. He was never the same again. Always passionate for the Master, nothing could ever dampen his zeal to win souls. He was a true evangelist. Many, many of his friends he personally led to the Lord, some of whom are in the ministry today.

Schooled under the hand of the old apostle, John Nelson Parr, Herbert was launched into full-time ministry as a travelling evangelist living in a caravan. So began a lifetime of service and a harvest of souls. Eventually finding himself conducting an evangelistic crusade in the northeast of England in Newcastle upon Tyne, he found his destiny. So began the Assemblies of God work in Newcastle.

The passion of the whole church was winning souls for Jesus. Herbert, a true evangelist, motivated the people to win their neighbours and their friends. The little boy who needed a father had found his heavenly Father and he wanted everyone else to do the same. Jesus was the answer to the despair and destruction of the world. The Father was gathering his spiritual orphans into his family. Herbert's church, Bethshan in Newcastle, grew to over seven hundred people.

Yet Herbert had a secret prayer, 'Lord, we have seen some measure of blessing in our lives and ministry, but oh Father, before I die, I long to be in a move of God. Let me live long enough to experience an awakening in your church and a harvest of souls.' From August 1994 when the Spirit of God broke out in our church, Herbert and Mary wanted to be at every meeting. Here was the answer to his longed-for prayer, 'Revive your church, oh Lord.' His heart thrilled as night after night he heard testimonies of lives changed and a passion for Jesus and the body of Christ erupting in heart after heart. Yet still he prayed, 'Lord, let us see a harvest of souls.'

Following the evening of our prophetic conference in September 1995 when, in truth, the fire fell, Herbert was thrilled at the harvest of young street kids, but his heart still cried for more, so, months later, he and Mary sat in a Boeing 747 headed for Buenos Aires to witness first-hand a revival. This is his story.

Herbert's story

'For twelve years Argentina has been in the throes of revival with millions turning to Christ. Churches that once were fifty-strong are now bursting at the seams, being forced to hold multiple services in buildings too small to hold the numbers coming in. It is reported that over the last two years two million people have come to Christ in Buenos Aires alone.

'September 1995 found my wife and me in Argentina to experience something of this astonishing move of God. It is difficult to know where to begin in describing the things we witnessed in the two weeks we spent there. But first it is important to note that Argentina experienced two phases of renewal. The first was accompanied by the kind of phenomena experienced by many in Britain over the last eighteen months but it died away because it failed to go beyond a self-serving, experience-centred thing. The second phase moved into kingdom-building harvest, after an intense time of repentance and intercession. An unknown businessman-turned-evangelist by the name of Carlos Anacondia spearheaded crusade-type events that ushered in hundreds of thousands of converts.

'In Argentina, as in the first-century church, several components make up the whole picture. These principles are now being adopted and worked out in Sunderland Christian Centre. It is all too easy to fasten on one single reason for the astonishing revival that hit Jerusalem in the first century. It was a sovereign work of God, says one. It was the outpouring of the Spirit at Pentecost, says another.

'In Argentina today, it is nearer the truth to say that whole cities are being evangelised and tens of thousands won for Jesus because of drastic changes of mindset and lifestyle. First, pastors are acknowledging that there is only one church in a town or city with one senior leader, the Lord Jesus Christ. The emphasis then becomes reaching the lost in the city with the gospel, regardless of which congregations they might join. In Argentina the spillover from the harvest is benefiting all the churches.

'Second, another component of the one-church concept is for pastors to cross denominational and ethnic barriers to begin to pray together, breaking the stronghold of disunity which has prevented us seeing the answer to our Lord's prayer in John 17:21, "that *all* of them be one . . . so that the world may believe that you have sent me". "When brothers live together in unity," Psalm 133 says, "the Lord bestows the blessing." Unity brings the anointing and it's the anointing that breaks the yoke of oppression in a city.

'We are seeing in Sunderland that God has called us to build *the* Church as well as a church. Already, several leaders across the denominations are meeting regularly for prayer in unity of heart and purpose – winning the lost. It is an exciting prospect.

'Third, in Argentina prayer has become a powerfully focused weapon. The nation as a whole, apparently, is engaged in a world-class power encounter. It is worth noting that since the renewal has moved us to prayer-evangelism with a day of prayer and fasting every Tuesday, beginning with a 6.30 a.m. men's intercessory time and scores of homes forming prayer cells in a chain throughout the day, and two hours of aggressive praying on a Saturday, people have been coming to Christ in almost every service.

'Fourth, prayer-evangelism provides the balance between God's sovereignty and human responsibility in winning the lost. Only God can save a soul but he has necessarily chosen human means to bring it to pass, apart from some exceptions as in the case of Paul's conversion (Acts 9, see 1 Corinthians 9:19–22). In Argentina it is not uncommon to see thousands coming together in a city to spend the night in prayer.'

Chapter 15

Heaven Comes Down

Robert Ward, an Anglican priest who attends Sunderland Christian Centre, led the visit to Argentina. He had many incredible things to share with us. This is his story.

Robert's story

'Argentina may have lost the war over the Falkland Islands, but they have gained their soul! For the country has been experiencing continuous revival ever since and one evangelist alone has led more than two million people to Christ. Thousands of churches have been planted and many of them have taken over theatres and cinemas and hold up to eight meetings a day, in at least one case moving to a football stadium for Sunday services. One church is entirely run by children while another is run by prison inmates.

'Economic collapse and national humiliation over the war seemed to have left a vacuum which God was able to fill but the foundation for much of what is happening has been the true love and unity amongst church leaders. This has led to a breaking-down of barriers and extraordinary reconciliation which has even influenced faraway Japan.

And one of the country's most notorious prisons now boasts a thousand-strong church of Spirit-filled believers – 50 per cent of the inmates – who are praying around the clock for the needs of each other and of the world outside.

'The background to my trip is that my good friend, Nick Cuthbert of Birmingham, had increased his awareness by the skilful use of tapes and books of the existence on earth of Ed Silvoso. Ed is an Argentinian ex-banker, brother-in-law of Luis Palau and Juan Carlos Ortiz and a highly gifted speaker, evangelist and teacher. He has been involved in the current revival in Argentina from its beginning thirteen years ago, and has established a worldwide ministry, teaching and helping implement the principles the revival is based on. Wherever these have been faithfully followed, by God's grace there has been much fruit in terms of accelerated church growth, Christian unity and general encouragement.

'The high spot of his ministry each year has been his annual international conference at which all the senior figures in the revival speak and teach, and their churches are invited while the growing number of delegates from around the world imbibe the spirit and vision of what God is doing in Latin America and take it home.

'I first met Ed at a conference at Ashburnham in Sussex over Christmas 1994 and invited him to lead his local conference on 'Taking your City for Christ' in Sunderland. Since August 1994, Sunderland has been a major centre of the renewal and thousands have visited us for refreshment. We felt that Ed's message would bring a clue about where these extraordinary times are leading. He came up to Sunderland with his excellent team and we were not disappointed. His clarity, humour and deep

82

Bible knowledge, combined with an appreciation of what God was doing in Argentina, truly won the hearts of each of the delegates.

'During the conference Ed publicly identified me as a "Spirit-filled wheeler-dealer" and challenged me to lead a party of UK folk to his annual international conference which is attended by some five hundred overseas delegates. "Robert, fifty will come, you'll see!" I smiled wanly, inwardly thinking the man to be mad, what with only six weeks to arrange it and with the summer holidays intervening and a £2,000 price tag attached to each trip!

'But six weeks later fifty-four UK delegates did indeed set off for what by general consent was the most amazing experience of their Christian lives. That they set off at all was due not only to Ed's faith, and God's grace, but to the hard work of another Birmingham friend, Jon Earnshaw, who spent his entire August helping folk register, answering their questions and holding their hand as they prepared to take their trip of a lifetime. The package I put together included arriving two days before the conference so we could adjust to the time zone, food, culture and begin to feel at home. This was a good move.

'Before World War II, Argentina was the sixth richest nation in the world. "The Argentine", as it was then known, produced beef and industrial goods which found a worldwide market. Populated predominantly by Spanish, but also by small numbers of Welsh people, Argentina truly enjoyed a golden age. Today, however, it is a Third World country. On arrival we were confronted by evidence of national collapse. Ships were literally rotting and rusting in the harbour which smelt like an open sewer. The centre of Buenos Aires, the capital, bore signs of terminal decay.

Their equivalent of Trafalgar Square was covered with generations of graffiti, the pavements were treacherously pot-holed and many of the vehicles belched smoke and were obviously not subjected to any kind of safety testing. Every taxi ride was itself a faith-building experience as the driving in Argentina is indeed terrifying.

'The background to Argentina's national collapse is the background to the Christian revival. It is as though the soul and pride of the nation was systematically broken so that their cry could rise to heaven. The national psyche of the Argentinians is apparently complex. Ed Silvoso told us that they have a confused identity. "They are," he said, "Spaniards who think like Italians, live like the French and wish they were English!" Eighty per cent of their forebears emigrated from Spain in search of streets paved with silver. ("Argentina" means "Land of Silver": just about the only thing the country does not have!)

'Argentina had put its trust in dictators – Peron and his wife Eva (as in "Don't cry for me, Argentina") were effectively worshipped. They eventually died, leaving a vast hole in the national soul. Then came crippling inflation which, at 1,000 per cent per annum, destroyed savings and all national wealth. Military dictatorship followed, with thousands of dissenters mysteriously "disappearing" in the night, never to return.

'Then, in 1982, in order to distract attention from mounting national disasters, the military junta invaded the Falklands. Every Argentinian has "Las Malvinas" engraved on their heart and so for a few dreadful weeks the government fed lie upon lie to the nation: "We are winning! The islands will soon be ours again!" Mrs Thatcher was seen as a woman of darkness whose task-force was being humiliated daily by the glorious sons of the motherland. Then the truth was revealed: Argentina had lost the war, the dictators had lied to the country and it was instead Argentina who had been humiliated before the whole world.

'The preparation for revival was complete. Just weeks after the Falklands defeat, news broke of an unheard-of preacher, a businessman called Carlos Anacondia, holding evangelistic rallies in towns and cities around the country. Reports told of ninety thousand converts here, seventy-five thousand there and a further eighty thousand elsewhere. Everywhere this man took his teams tens of thousands responded, and there were reports of exorcisms and miraculous healings. Today conservative estimates are that Anacondia has led over two million to Christ and seen them established in local churches, themselves led by "children" of the revival.

'For the last thirteen years the revival has continued. Thousands of churches have been planted, many of them thousands strong. The city-centre churches typically buy old theatres and cinemas (built in Argentina's golden age) which comfortably hold two thousand. Several of the larger churches hold multiple services each day. One church we attended at 11 p.m. was effervescently led by the same man who had begun his day eight meetings earlier! On Sunday he just takes the service in the football stadium.

'Each evening we visited churches or what I suppose could be "religious sites" of a kind where heaven came down! On one evening we visited a children's church. Attached to the main fellowship, this consists entirely of children aged three to sixteen led by youth leaders in their teens. The meeting lasted three-and-a-half hours. The intercession was breathtaking. An eight-year-old, for example, prayed fervently for about ten minutes obviously led by the Holy Spirit, with weeping, punctuated only by the cries and "Amens" of the other four hundred children, a number of whom prayed after him. Then we "foreigners", as we were referred to, were invited forward for prayer. As we knelt down, dozens of little hands patted and stroked us with soft whispers in tongues, pleadings to God and joyful prayer and many of us – now on our faces – received the touch of God through these precious channels. I suppose this lasted twenty minutes – an amazing time.

'We rose, to be told that in a day or two's time this mighty army of tiny warriors would be visiting patients in the local children's hospital. Here they would be praying for the sick. Over recent years, hundreds of children have been miraculously healed. There are thick files detailing each healing medically – these are kept in the office of what they call the Department of Miracles! When a sceptical television producer set about disparaging this work in a TV documentary, his "devil's advocates" were dumbfounded when faced with this amazing evidence. Before millions of viewers they had no choice but to admit this had to be God! Naturally the Church grew substantially as a result of this glorifying programme!

'Contrast this fresh innocence with the restored innocence we met on our visit to Olmos Prison, the largest and hitherto most dreaded high security prison in Argentina. Before the revival such management as it knew was at the hands of the Mafia and drug barons who were permitted to run it by the exasperated and defeated prison staff. It was a terrible place. Vastly overcrowded, it was the scene of bestial occult sacrifices, widespread homosexual rapes and gang warfare. It would have made Frankland Prison, a high security jail near Durham where I was a chaplain until recently, seem a high-class finishing school!

'Now Olmos has over a thousand powerfully converted Spirit-filled prisoners, fully 50 per cent of the total prison population. The Christians now run the prison instead of the Mafia, many of whose former members are themselves gloriously redeemed. We were invited to attend a chapel meeting. A thousand convicts (separated from us only by a thin rope with not a guard in sight) worshipped God with electrifying praise – their faces, many bearing the scars of their former lifestyle, now radiant, joyful and determined to honour their God and saviour. There are five pastors, the senior pastor confessing to having been the most vicious persecutor of the Christians when the Spirit first moved in the place.

'Now the Christians occupy several of the prison wings. Only those whose life and witness is wholehearted can join the Christian community, where there is round-the-clock prayer and intercession. At night, teams pray for the inmates as they sleep and by day intercession fuels the national revival. We were invited to leave our prayer requests with the pastors for the inmates to attend to later. Seldom have I seen Christians write such comprehensive and focused requests!

'Such is the respect and awe in which the Christians are held in the prison that hundreds of inmates apply to live in the Christian quarters. Not surprisingly, there is always a waiting-list to join what I suppose is the most fruitful "monastic" lifestyle I have ever glimpsed. Such is the reputation of Olmos in the prison network – 98 per cent of released prisoners have yet to re-offend – that the governors of Argentina's other prisons constantly request transfers of Olmos Christians to influence their establishments. Hence the revival in the prisons is spreading nationwide.

'Incidentally, the revival in Olmos began when an evangelical pastor was given a prison sentence for theft. After he had repented God used him to preach the gospel and, helped by a Christian warder, the exciting harvest began.

'As we travelled from place to place, we noticed that the repertoire of songs sung was small – maybe a dozen different songs seemed to be in vogue but they were vehicles to bring us into God's presence. The main thrust was God's glory, Jesus's victory over Satan, our freedom in Christ and the power of the Spirit. There was an absolute certainty of God's presence with us, a clear expectation that he would bless and empower us, and a thrilling knowledge that we were part of a glorious army experiencing campaign victory after campaign victory. The church leaders we met and watched "in the saddle" all had an authority before God and their people which was almost tangible and yet a childlike lightness of spirit and sense of fun which was infectious. This helped me realise that they were not dictators but men who were known and trusted by their people, their peers – and evidently by God.

'Wherever we went, we "foreigners" were treated with unfeigned love and warmth. It is the Argentinian way for men to kiss men. This terrifying tactile experience met some resistance from us at first (garlic and whiskers do not appeal to the natural man nor his deeper inclinations). But we soon behaved in a culturally relevant way and our clever sophisticated battle-weary Western hearts were softened by the embrace and affection of those lovely people, most of whom were in darkness a few years ago and yet now seemed to enjoy signs of freedom some of us have only dreamed about.

'On the last full day of the conference Ed Silvoso

arranged a special event for us: an enormous barbecue where whole cattle were roasted on huge fires, split down the middle and pegged open on screens. Quite disturbing visually but very tasty in bite-sized chunks. These were served to us by "gauchos", Argentinian cowboys who are national hero figures from Argentina's golden age. Whenever they brought in the food – Argentine steak is surely the best and biggest in the whole world – huge cheers and choruses went up from our hosts. The barbecue is a special event in Argentina and ours outdid them all. After the meal there was a demonstration of national dancing by the gauchos and their lady counterparts.

'This was all very entertaining and hugely enjoyable. Afterwards we delegates – five hundred of us from all over the world, dazed and replete – mingled with hundreds of Argentinian pastors and their wives. But the best was about to come ... The Argentinians were directed to stand in two long rows and join hands to form an enormous tunnel through which we foreigners all trooped to the strains of "When the saints go marching in"! As we passed through, the Argentinian pastors and their wives embraced us, laid hands on us and prayed for us. Several of us fell under the power of the Spirit and had to be carried through, but for the rest it was a conscious experience of the boundless love of God, a feeling of transparent joy and a childlike revelling in the presence of our heavenly Father. It was also a delightful realisation of Holy Spirit community, of being truly one in Christ.

'Before long we were climbing aboard the British Airways 747–400, the largest plane ever to enter passenger service. From my window seat I could see the wing tips flapping, as though the Boeing company was returning to a more traditional flight technology. "Don't worry," the captain told me, "the wings generally flap a little. Up to 20ft is quite normal on a rough runway like Buenos Aires. They only snap off at 40ft."

'As we and the wings settled down for the thirteen-hour flight back to Heathrow, we began to discuss among ourselves and reflect before God what it was that our lovely hosts had discovered; the secrets, if you will, of one of the longest-running revivals of the twentieth century. For one thing, Ed Silvoso told us, it was not deserved. In the 1970s, Juan Carlos Ortiz and his book *Disciple* came out of an earlier awakening when many were converted. But, said Ed, the Church messed it up by saying in effect that the manifestations of the Spirit's power meant that the Bible wasn't as necessary as before. For a time the evangelical Church lost direction as this move of God fizzled out. Then, entirely by his grace, the Lord gave the Argentinian Christians a second chance.

'The second secret is a profound awareness of spiritual warfare. Carlos Anacondia, in his address to the conference, began by saying: "We must know our enemy in order to defeat him. Remember 1 John 5:19 – we know we are of God and the whole world lies in the power of the evil one." "Recognise the truth of this," he continued. "Sometimes it seems not to be true, but it is: as for us, we know we are of God, protected by God."

'In the Western Church today we hardly mention the devil. Yet Scripture says, "We are not ignorant of his devices." After Argentina I realised how ignorant we are and how silly we have become in not recognising and addressing devilish strategy. During the conference a high proportion of delegates fell prey to some illness or other and I myself felt oppressed for several days and was indeed grateful to those at home who were praying for me.

'The third secret is true unity. The foundation of what Ed calls "city-taking" – seeking to win whole communities for Christ – is real, genuine, transparent love and unity between the leaders of congregations in a community. Note: *congregations*. What the Argentinian church leaders have discovered is the biblical truth that in a community there is one Church (led by Jesus) with many congregations led by under-shepherds, that is, pastors. As barriers, prejudices, fearfully held "distinctives" and suspicions are abandoned to God's love, the true body of Christ is discerned and the Church is granted authority in the heavenly places. She can now conduct effective warfare against the powers and principalities which bind and blind the souls and social structures of the community where the local church with its many congregations may rule with Christ according to his revealed will.

'Part of this has to do with "spiritual mapping" – an understanding of the spiritual history of a community. Knowing the history helps in prayer strategy. For example, one of the Argentine dictators appointed a sorcerer to his inner circle. He cursed the land and the crops failed, speeding economic failure. Armed with this insight, the Christians were able to break the curse on the land by the grace of God, restoring agricultural prosperity.

'The American intercessor, Cindi Jacobs, has been a key figure in this area. Her testimony is that one night the Lord appeared to her in a vision and said, "I will bring revival to Argentina. In case you don't think it is me, get in touch with your friend (indicating a particular person) and she will confirm my word." Cindi lost no time contacting her friend who had had a similar visitation shortly before.

Immediately Cindi committed herself wholeheartedly to the work of God in Argentina. She prayed individually with each of us during the conference as she had, shall we say, a high degree of "pulpit cred"!

'Fourth, the secret of reconciliation. This is closely connected with unity. For example, a high spot for all the international delegates was listening to Dr Paul Ariga, the Japanese answer to Reinhard Bonnke. A tiny man of irrepressible energy, he irritated me enormously at first. But I quickly realised that just below the surface I had a suspicious and despising attitude towards the Japanese character, obviously connected with their war record and business practices. Nevertheless, the Holy Spirit convicted me of my hateful spirit and I had an opportunity of praying with him before he spoke to us.

'Imagine my feelings, therefore, when he stood and confessed the sins of Japan to us and begged our forgiveness for their war crimes down the years. He invited the Japanese contingent of about two dozen to stand and asked us to pray with them. There were loud cries and weeping as hundreds of us not only forgave the Japanese but also confessed our hardness of heart towards them. It was truly a miraculous reconciliation. God has greatly blessed Dr Ariga. Since his first visit to Ed Silvoso's conference three years ago he has planted ninety churches in Japan! He lives in Kobi where the disastrous earthquake struck last year. Shortly before it happened a prophetic warning came, as a result of which the Christians chose not to sleep indoors that night and escaped the devastations.

'As we touched down at Heathrow we all knew we'd touched, tasted and glimpsed something we'd longed to understand for years. I'd been hearing that "revival is just around the corner" ever since my conversion in 1972. But to have seen around the Argentinian corner was amazing: mountains of new disciples, transformed prisons, consistent exponential growth and profound biblical understanding among even young believers. All very illuminating and rather humbling. In fact at times I began (for a short moment) to wonder how converted I really was! To breathe the air of revival, to be loved and received as we were by the children and leaders of revival was wonderful. To be with those who live under an open heaven, those who understand something of the sovereignty of God as well as the responsibility of a man and who are living in the good and the fullness of it was . . . well, like being on another planet! It really was a special time which I am sure will have far-reaching consequences for us and the work we do.'

Chapter 16

A Timely Visit

While ministering in Brisbane in October 1995, we received a telephone call to ask whether our good friends Melody and Andy Seivright could come and visit us in Sunderland the day after we returned home. Melody was tragically widowed when her husband, Keith Green, went to be with the Lord, along with two of their precious children, Josiah and Bethany, in the early 1980s. After incredibly triumphing over that desperate tragedy, Melody fell in love with Andy and they became husband and wife.

We first met them in Toronto. Andy is a precious godly man with a wonderfully gracious spirit and a strong prophetic anointing, and Melody is a woman utterly obedient to the Father. We felt an immediate connection in the spirit and I knew that somehow these two people would be part of what God was doing in Sunderland. As a young man the Lord had spoken to Andy and told him he would be used somehow, somewhere in the future, in England.

So, we were delighted that our friends were coming to visit. In some ways we wished they could have come when we weren't so jet-lagged, when we had taken the opportunity to settle back into our church life, when it wasn't snowing so hard. But God sent them in his perfect time.

94

We had returned from Australia to find an atmosphere of change in the church. Having taught on prayer and evangelism for four weeks, both Herbert and the people had hearts to 'go for the lost and go for the worst'. A sense of new beginnings was in the air.

As we took Mel and Andy to lunch in an old castle, now a hotel, Ken was questioning in his mind, 'Lord, what are you saying? What do you want us to do? We know you are showing us the way Lord but please show it clearly. We don't want to make mistakes. We've been a world renewal centre now for over a year. You've done something with our hearts and you're urging us to move on. Give us clear direction.' At that precise moment Andy leaned over from the back of the car, tapped him on the shoulder and said, 'Ken, perhaps you need to link up now with some of our YWAM friends to help you, because a prayer strategy is next for the taking of your city.' We were stunned. It was like hearing the audible voice of the Lord. 'This is the way, walk ye in it.'

Inevitably we got to talking about Keith, a man ahead of his time, burning with the Holy Spirit, passionate for the lost, filled with compassion for the poor, and revealing a love for Jesus. His message, so adequately conveyed in his wonderful songs, had a new relevance for us in the light of all the Holy Spirit had done in our hearts. As Melody stood that evening and sang, 'There is a Redeemer', one of the songs she wrote herself, the tears streamed down my cheeks. They also coursed down someone else's cheeks too. One of our region's toughest underworld criminals, unknown to us, was in our service, gun in his pocket, to see why some of his colleagues had been so radically changed. With tears he accepted prayer from my father, Herbert.

Later that evening, Mel, Andy, Ken and myself spent some time in prayer together. It was precious and profound. The Father was speaking to our hearts through Mel and Andy. Something was being imparted we didn't understand until much later. None of us were aware of the significance of that time in God's presence.

'Lord,' Andy prayed, 'Ken and Lois sense something in their spirits. They know you are asking them to move forward, but it's uncharted territory. No-one can show them the model of what you want them to do, they just have to blindly follow. Help them hear your voice and have the courage to be obedient.' That precious couple blew a wonderful prophetic breeze through our lives, imparted to us something of their own hearts, and revealed to us more of Jesus. We love them dearly and we know they will play yet a greater part in the development of God's path for our lives and our nation.

The Lord used that short timely visit to push us further upstream. We never dreamed what lay ahead.

Chapter 17

Strategies for the City

General Booth was moved by the compassion of Christ to do something about this world. The Bible recounts the story of a similar man, Nehemiah, the cup bearer to Artaxerxes, governor of Jerusalem after Zerubbabel. Nehemiah asked questions about his homeland such that when the answers came they devastated him. The walls of Jerusalem had broken down and the gates were burned with fire. The news caused him such distress he wept, prayed, fasted and mourned for days.

If we were to ask questions about our society, would the answers cause us to be so disturbed we would lose sleep? The walls of our cities are down and the gates are burning. In one day, today, even in the United States alone five thousand will try cocaine for the first time. Two thousand will start using crack. Some 3.3 million American teenagers are alcoholics. In one ten-minute period, ten American kids will attempt suicide, 105 kids will leave school, 618 high-school seniors will smoke marijuana. Twenty girls between the ages of fiteen and nineteen will become pregnant, five of whom will have illegitimate babies, eight will have abortions.[1]

---

1. Dr David J. Seifert, Modesto, California, *Bible Illustrator for Windows*.

One teenager wrote to a national newspaper and asked the older generation a few questions. Are your parents divorced? Almost every one of my friends comes from a broken home. Were you thinking of suicide when you were twelve years old? Did you have an ulcer when you were sixteen? Did your best friend lose her virginity to a young man she went out with twice? Did you have to worry about AIDS? Did your classmates carry guns and knives? How many kids in your class came to school regularly drunk, stoned or high on drugs? What percentage of your graduating class also graduated from a drug and alcohol rehabilitation centre?[2]

Have these situations disturbed us as much as they did General Booth and Nehemiah? When a man with a gun can walk into a primary school in a little village in Scotland and shoot dead sixteen children and one teacher, and seriously wound others, does that cause you to weep, mourn and fast for days? Sometimes our eyes are too dry and our hearts too hard.

The late J. Edwin Orr says, 'Whenever God is ready to do something new with his people, he always sets them to praying.'[3] As a modern authority on revival, Orr believed that the early twentieth-century worldwide evangelical awakening did not begin with the Welsh revival of 1904–5. Rather, its sources were in the springs of little prayer meetings which seemed to arise spontaneously all over the world, combining into the streams of expectation which became a river of

2. *Bible Illustrator for Windows*.
3. Edwin Orr, *The Flaming Tongue: The Impact on Twentieth Century Revival* (Moody Press, Chicago, 1973), pp. 1–28.

blessing in which the Welsh revival became the great catalyst.

Interestingly, over four years ago I took our prayer meeting into the streets of Sunderland. I felt led to take the church week after week to a spot surrounded by night-clubs. Stretching out their hands, the people asked the Lord to save the men who ran these places and the girls who were dancing, scantily dressed. Incredibly, Jim Richardson was right there at the time. Marie, his wife, was a dancer. Prayer works! What began as a 'voice in the wilderness' calling the Church to united prayer has now become a roar louder than Niagara Falls. *Newsweek* wrote in its article 'Talking to God', 'This week, if you believe at all in opinion surveys, more of us will pray than will go to work, exercise, or have sexual relations.' Bryant cites David Barrett, the leading demographer of world Christian movement as saying:

1. Worldwide there are about 170 million Christians who are committed to praying every day for spiritual awakening and world evangelisation.
2. Of these, twenty million believe that praying in that direction is their primary calling in ministry within the body of Christ (what we might otherwise call 'prayer warriors').
3. Worldwide there are at least ten million prayer groups that have as a major focus every time they meet to pray to seek God for a coming world revival.

And finally,

4. Worldwide there are an estimated thirteen hundred prayer mobilisation networks that are seeking to stir up the church to accelerated prayer for world revival and mission.[4]

Examples of this are everywhere, private and public. They may be bold and visible like 1994's 'A Day to Change the World' which saw the greatest co-ordination of humankind in history as an estimated thirty million Christians prayed in unison over a 24–hour period for the closure of the Great Commission by the year 2000. Or, the 'flagpole prayer movement', as two million high-school students in America gather around their flagpoles on the first day of school to intercede for revival on their campuses. Or, Promise Keepers' desire to bring one million men together in Washington DC in 1996, among other things to pray for national revival.

The Lord has drawn our hearts to himself, but again and again we are hearing the Lord say, 'Whom shall I send, and who will go for us?' Then I said, 'Here am I, send me.' Dwight L. Moody implored of the Father, 'Use me, then, my saviour, for whatever purpose and in whatever way thou mayest require. Here is my poor heart an empty vessel; fill it with thy grace.'[5]

As Nehemiah moved to do something about the situation of his people and rebuild the walls, his enemies laughed at him. For too long the Church of Jesus Christ has made too small an impact in this present world. George Verwer wrote a humorous adaptation

4. David Bryant, *The Hope at Hand* (Baker Books, Grand Rapids, 1995), p. 27.
5. D. L. Moody, 'Baptism in the Spirit', in J. G. Lawson (ed.), *Deeper Experiences of Famous Christians* (Warner Press, 1911), pp. 245–9.

of the hymn 'Onward Christian soldiers' to illustrate
this.

Backward Christian soldiers fleeing from the fight,
With the cross of Jesus clearly out of sight:
Christ our rightful Master stands against the foe
But forward into battle we are chicken to go.

Like a mighty tortoise moves the Church of God;
Brothers we are treading where we've often trod,
We are much divided, many bodies we,
Having different doctrines, not much charity.

Crowns and thrones may perish, kingdoms rise and
wane,
But the Church of Jesus hidden does remain;
Gates of hell should never 'gainst that Church prevail,
We have Christ's own promise, but think that it
will fail.

Sit here, then, ye people, join our useless throng;
Blend with ours your voices in a feeble song.
Blessings, ease, and comfort, ask from Christ the
King.
With our modern thinking, we won't do a thing.[6]

Like an irresistible siren's call, the Holy Spirit is wooing
his worshippers everywhere to prayer.

John and Carol Arnott, frustrated with doing it on their
own power for so many years, decided in 1993 to give their

6. George Verwer, *Come! Live! Die!* pp. 91–2.

mornings to God. They spent most of their mornings all that year in personal prayer and devotion to the Lord.

Yongi Cho, pastor of the largest church in the world, when asked the secret of his success replied, 'I pray and I obey.'

Nehemiah risked everything – his job, his freedom and even his life – to do something about the situation. The reality is that when your heart has been affected you will risk everything to change your world and repair the walls and gates of your society. We have found to our surprise here in Sunderland our hearts have been so deeply affected as the Holy Spirit has been poured out in this move of God, we are ready to risk all to rebuild the walls of our city.

As Nehemiah began to repair the walls of Jerusalem Sanballat and Tobiah began to get angry. They laughed and despised Nehemiah. Many will laugh at us too, but Psalm 2:4 declares: 'The One enthroned in heaven laughs, the Lord scoffs at them.' I think the Psalmist is saying he who sits in the heavens shall have the last laugh. After using the weapons of laughter and ridicule, the enemies of Nehemiah became very angry. The Christian life is a fight, not just an occasional skirmish, and you will remain in a battle until you reach heaven.

1 Corinthians 9:16 says, 'Yet when I preach the gospel, I cannot boast, for I am compelled to preach. Woe to me if I do not preach the gospel!' 1 Timothy 6:12 says, 'Fight the good fight of the faith. Take hold of the eternal life to which you were called when you made your good confession in the presence of many witnesses.' 2 Timothy 4:7 says, 'I have fought the good fight, I have finished the race, I have kept the faith.'

John Wimber has said that unless we are up-front with people when they come to Christ, they can come into the kingdom with all kinds of false expectations, especially if our preaching suggests that if you come to Christ you will have no more problems.

Let me ask all of you Christian readers, who has never had a problem since they got saved? None of us! However, we now have One who walks through the problem with us.

If we are not up-front then people come to Christ as if they were about to embark on some world cruise. They stroll up wearing Bermuda shorts, carrying towels and sun cream. Unfortunately when they arrive at the dock they see not the cruiser of their dreams, but a warship, with guns and crew at battle stations. When you become a Christian you have enlisted and your place in the battle is the front line. 1 Peter 5:8–11 reads,

> Be self-controlled and alert. Your enemy the devil prowls around like a roaring lion looking for someone to devour. Resist him, standing firm in the faith, because you know that your brothers throughout the world are undergoing the same kind of sufferings. And the God of all grace, who called you to his eternal glory in Christ, after you have suffered a little while, will himself restore you and make you strong, firm and steadfast. To him be the power for ever and ever. Amen.

Nehemiah 4:9 says, 'But we prayed to our God and posted a guard day and night to meet this threat.' We need watchmen who can give revelation as to the enemy's strategy, intercessors who will pray day and night guarding and protecting God's people and bring deliverance to our cities.

Evangelist Reinhard Bonnke often recounts the story

of a time when he was desperately sick in Africa with a fever. All he could do was cry out to Jesus. Meanwhile, back home in Germany a woman was woken by the Holy Spirit and felt an incredible burden to pray for Reinhard. As she prayed in Germany, he recovered in Africa. The body of Christ needs watchmen.

Nehemiah's response to the attacks of the enemy was to simply ask God to take care of it and get on with the work. He simply gave it to God and got on with the job. He and the people had a mind to work. Do you have a mind to work? I pray so.

In Sunderland we began to pray fervently. With our hearts changed by twenty months of soaking in the presence of the Lord, we began to seek his face like never before. Always a praying church, we started again in earnest. Every Tuesday morning at six, every Saturday evening, and prayer and fasting every Tuesday with a 24-hour chain of continuous prayer. Quite sovereignly the Holy Spirit led our prayer along a specific path.

A group of Germans praying with us spontaneously began to weep and I noticed an old lady with white hair, sobbing among them. I felt the Holy Spirit asking me to do something and I was immediately obedient. 'I want the German people to come forward,' I said, and, taking the old lady by the hand, I looked into her face and as the tears flowed, I asked the Germans and that dear old lady in particular, if they could possibly forgive us British as a nation for the death and hatred that had existed between us. Crying out in anguish, the old lady sank to her knees and began to shout out in German. The interpreter moved forward and taking a microphone began to translate:

'I am from Dresden. My city was destroyed by the British. I watched as truck-loads of our dead sons and fathers were carried from our city. I watched as my own sons were carried out. Today the Lord has lifted the anger and hurt from my heart. Now, could you English please forgive all that our nation Germany did to you? Please forgive us.' The old lady stopped sobbing. The Germans stood in a frozen moment, and out from the congregation streamed the British to take them in their arms and weep as each nation asked forgiveness of the other. What a moment! Walls were coming down. Out from the crowd stepped a Jewish family, and taking the Germans – as many as they could get in their arms – they wept in repentance and reconciliation.

Then a young German pastor took the microphone, and prayed in his own language for God's blessing on the United Kingdom. Where there had been a spirit of hatred, enmity, murder and division, we were defeating it with the opposite spirit of love, repentance, compassion and unity. A beautiful young Australian girl took the microphone and, weeping, she confessed her hatred of the Japanese, since her father had been killed in a Japanese prisoner-of-war camp. A young Asian girl took her in her arms and ministered the comfort of Jesus. This scene has been played out many times over the last six months in Sunderland Christian Centre.

As the IRA bombing campaign once again commenced in London and lives were lost, we had both Northern and Southern Irish in our service. Once again I called them forward. There was repentance, reconciliation and united prayer which shook the heavens. It is not unusual to find, in our prayer services every Saturday evening, Poles praying in Polish, Norwegians, Dutch, French and Australians, participating in corporate prayer in unity, breaking the strongholds of division. The prayer meeting is both the most exciting and powerful meeting to attend. And it produced the breakthrough.

I began to lead everyone in a prayer of thanks for our cities – whichever city we had come from. I urged everyone not to join hands with the enemy and agree with the negatives we saw in our cities, but agree with God, and thank him for his divine purpose for them. We began to thank God for the heritage of revival in Sunderland and praise him for his purposes for it. The city had seen wonderful breakthroughs with Moody and Sankey, with the Jeffries brothers and Alexander Boddy. It was the city where revival broke out and Smith Wigglesworth was baptised in the Holy Spirit. Yet our city had always known spiritual division as had, I am sure, every other town and city in our nation.

The Argentinians had given us some clear prayer strategy. As well as prayer homes where our congregation were engaged in continuous prayer for neighbours and family, prayer chains and days of fasting, the greatest strategy was the spiritual leadership of a city coming together for united heartfelt prayer. This was not meant to be a fraternity but a coming together of people whose hearts have laid down pride, competition and suspicion and have come together to extend the kingdom. Again we were reminded of Nehemiah, the walls are down, the gates are hung. Did it concern us? Yes it did.

Ed Silvoso had said in a city where there is 10 per cent unity there is 10 per cent power. Where there is 50 per cent unity there is 50 per cent power. He went even further, saying, 'Every time we don't deal with a broken relationship we are dabbling with the demonic.'

Where there has been threat, hostility and division in our city, my heart cried for unity. The Lord asked Ken and me to repent of many of the attitudes we had had since we came into Sunderland and to ask forgiveness of leaders of other churches for our manner towards them. So, they began, one or two at first, to pray together once a week. It began slowly and added men one by one, stage by stage. We were to see a phenomenal breakthrough almost immediately.

David Brown, a pastor in Sunderland from a different denomination, travelled to Argentina with Herbert and Mary. He and Herbert decided on their return to pray in unity for our city. This is his story.

David's story

'World revival has always stirred something in my being, but I never dreamed that one day I would stand awestruck in a country that is experiencing revival following years of spiritual decay. Argentina, twelve years ago, had fewer than 1 per cent who would claim to be "born again". It now expects by the year 2000 to have an estimated 60 per cent of the population "born again". They are certainly seeing something of the wonderful church growth similar to that recorded in the book of the Acts of the Apostles.

'But how did this journey to Argentina begin? In late June 1995 a group led by an Argentinian evangelist called Ed Silvoso held a seminar at Sunderland Christian Centre. The title was "Preparing our Region for Revival". We were drawn by the thought of true revival. Over these three days we learned some of the principles used in Argentina and now around the world to reach cities with the life-changing message of Jesus. Having taken part in many outreaches during the last twenty-five years and with minimal results in reaching the lost, it was uplifting and yet challenging that whole cities in Argentina are being affected. Even so, these seminars didn't prepare us for what we would see some months later. At the leaders' lunch on the last day of the seminars in Sunderland, Ed Silvoso extended an invitation to go to Argentina in October to the "Harvest Evangelism Institute". Details were promised later. As the details became available I experienced a time of real questioning. Should my wife and I go or not? I'm really glad we did because it proved to be a life-changing experience.

'In those ten days so much happened it is difficult to even decide what was the highest point. Was it Olmos Prison where 1,600 of 3,000 inmates now belong to an intercessors' church? Was it the Buenos Aires March for Jesus where true repentance took place between Argentinian young people and English believers? Was it the church service that lasted until 1.45 a.m., with much of the day of Pentecost repeated in our midst? Was it the church in Mar Del Plata that reaches between 1,500 and 2,000 people a week? Was it the Baptist church that grew from 250 to 4,500 in three years? Was it the Argentinian evangelist who has led two million people to Christ in eight years? Was it the Argentinian apostle who has planted 132 churches in ten years? Was it the young Argentinian pastor who raised a young boy from the dead at his funeral service?

'Was it the heavy sense of the presence of the Holy Spirit in all the meetings? Was it the gold fillings in teeth, put there by the Divine Dentist, or even the people who had walked on water? Was it the wonderful Christ-like love the Argentinian believers showered upon us? Was it my personal deliverance from a ten-generation forefathers' link with freemasonry? Was it seeing the power of the

Lord's presence come on many of the fifty-four visitors from the United Kingdom to the Institute, or even the church which has child intercessors who take the service once a month, some of the children only eight years old? Was it the Department of Miracles run by the church doctors where every miracle is documented – "before" and "after" medical details? Was it the wonderful freedom there is in the praise in Argentine churches? Or was it the city-taking strategy that we had now seen as well as heard?

'It is certainly possible we in England will see all of this if we target our cities for God in the way they have in Argentina. In my own case this would be the city of Sunderland.

'Sunderland was well represented in Argentina and Herbert Harrison and I made a commitment that we would begin to follow the Argentine model when we arrived back home. The whole strategy is based in prayer and begins with the pastors in a city gathering together for open and honest prayer and fellowship, dealing with felt needs and seeking to bring about a unity as members of the one-time Church of Jesus Christ. The scriptural basis for this is in Psalm 113 and John 17:20–3. In fact, I personally wonder at the thought that Jesus, in his heavenly intercessory role, is still praying that prayer for us now. The verse that has the greatest impact on me personally is verse 21: "that all of them may be one, Father, just as you are in me and I am in you. May they also be in us so that the world may believe that you have sent me." I find that a truly motivating verse of Scripture.

'One of the truths received whilst in Argentina came from the book of Joel. In chapter 2 between verses 12 and 17 is a call to the church to repentance, individually and corporately. I believe the power in the Argentinian Church began here with repentance from division, competitiveness and our narrow-minded pride-filled hearts. This is similar to the Scripture in Acts 3:19. As ministers come together to pray, they open their hearts and make themselves vulnerable to each other and to the Holy Spirit. Eventually this pattern will extend to their churches and the whole city.

'Early 1996 saw three pastors gather for prayer and to seek the Lord. Now it has grown to six and we will add others as the Holy Spirit directs us. Eventually invitations will go out to every minister in the city to come and join in the prayer breakthrough. We are walking steadily. None of us has been this route before but we are sure that it will lead to a mighty breakthrough in our city, not Buenos Aires but Sunderland. This, of course, can be any city where the Church will unite.

'Finally, about England and that desire for revival to come to our nation, my personal belief is that "It is now God's time for our nation and we must work while it is daylight because the night cometh." Yes, truly England will be revived.'

Chapter 18

Changing the Wineskins

It became obvious towards the end of 1995 that we needed to make some changes to our wineskins. Street kids were turning up night after night whilst we were running renewal services. They physically needed room to grow and be spiritually fed. Then a thought struck home to my heart. 'Ken,' I said, 'when God broke into our lives we did not tag renewal onto the end of our services. We fully embraced all that the Father was doing. Now that he has sent harvest, we can't tag that on the end of our renewal. We must embrace what the Father is doing and so embrace the harvest that we have longed for.' Renewal cost us in terms of our time, our facility, our programmes, our structure, our finance and much more. The harvest I believe, will cost us in very much the same way. Therefore there has to be a certain amount of investment.

The investment into a field of wheat is a sack of grain. That grain could have been ground up into more flour for more bread. Without the investment there would be no field of wheat the following year.

Renewal meant a whole new wineskin in relation to our programmes in order to accommodate the new wine. I know the harvest will mean that we will need to be just

111

as flexible. We were about to re-programme again. We had to restructure to accommodate the huge amount of visitors coming to us. Now we felt the need to restructure for the harvest, to accommodate all the new converts that God was about to send.

The visitors who still flocked from home and abroad were to be channelled into many new things. They began to see a model from renewal into harvest, with prayer being a primary focus. We decided after a great deal of prayer and heart-searching to cut two nights from our renewal programme and give the street kids two nights in our building for their own services. Visitors coming were shown the wonderful things happening in these young people's lives.

It was also apparent that our church structures were in need of total overhaul. The people were hurting. Our church of two hundred and thirty people had grown to well over five hundred people. We were and still are holding conferences for many thousands of people and we were running renewal services every night. Ken and I were ministering away now far more than we had ever done before. In addition, the street kids were coming in and needed time, care and love. After all, we had prayed for this for a long time. All this was happening with the leaders we had had pre-renewal. The church needed care. The people needed shepherds. However, in the restructuring, in order to accommodate such growth we saw incredible evidence of the fruits of the Holy Spirit in hearts.

At that time we had just one full-time pastor who had only been brought onto staff a few months previously. Myself and two elders with demanding secular jobs completed the team. One man in particular, Jim Elliott, had been at my husband's side from the founding of the church in Sunderland. He is a practical man of integrity and character and yet with prophetic insight and purpose. He was Ken's right arm and yet he had a fear. Jim knew that he had never received a call into full-time ministry, and he was afraid he would be asked to do just that. He is also a man of integrity and was aware that his secular employment was so demanding it left little time for the work of God, especially in the explosion of things as they now were.

Then there was myself, confident on the platform, happy to minister publicly by my husband's side. I had also been fulfilling a role in the church that had been an increasing burden I knew I was not called to do. I wanted to be released and had done so for over a year. Headship and government burdened and distressed me. My husband needed co-workers.

Nick Hiscott, our other elder, a sensitive and prophetic man of the Spirit, and incredibly gifted graphic designer, had, since a visit to Toronto, known God was calling him back to his roots. He was from London. With joy and blessing we released him to his calling.

Prior to leaving for ministry in Australia in the autumn of 1995, Jim Elliott remained behind in our home after a meeting to speak with us. 'Ken,' he said. 'I've always wanted to serve and be useful and never stand in the way as God moves us on. I have helped, I have supported, but I am a dabbler. I've dabbled in things that now need specialists, full-time specialists. The people need to be pastored and I am prepared to stand aside so that someone with a specialist gift from God can take my place. I don't have the time you need from me to give to all the demands. God has brought in men with a call and with time. Do not let your feelings for me or sentiment get in the way of what God wants to do.'

We were so moved by his words, and I could see why he was a man God had used so powerfully in our development as a church. Truly he is a big man in the Spirit and here in this book I would like to honour him. Apart from Jim, the one who worked closest to Ken was me. Happy to share the platform at home and all over the world, I had been feeling what Jim had just expressed. At home in ministry, uncomfortable in government. I wanted to be released and Jim's words echoed my own.

So, we set off for Australia to pray about these things and stayed in the home of Phil Hills from Melbourne. He encouraged us to make faith decisions on our return and expand the team with full-time men who could help pastor the flock, and expand and develop the church God had given us. So when we returned, Jim and Nick and I stood down, in love preferring others who, with their gifts, were about to add to our church. They were able to do so because of the humility and adaptability of others.

The Lord had also touched our hearts concerning children's ministries. Those who had been to Argentina had seen a children's church in operation: little ones praying for the sick, interceding and leading meetings. We were striving to do the same here. The Lord is putting together a wonderful team so that a children's church can be established. The wineskins had been changed. God was about to pour in new wine.

Chapter 19

The Harvest Begins

When the lost began to come into our church in numbers, we found it was a sovereign move, and began as suddenly and spontaneously as renewal had done. It was as if God had been soaking a large sponge for nearly two years with his Holy Spirit and we had become totally saturated. Then the hand of God began to squeeze the sponge and from it rivers began to flow out in the most unexpected places. We were also praying in unity for our city. Our building, which had seen nightly renewal services, was now filled night and day. We had been so amazed when we heard of 23–hour church in Argentina, and yet now in our own building as one shift moved out another moved in. Like revivals of old God began to sovereignly move in the poorer communities. The street kids who came to meet with Jim and Marie were first. Every evening they turned up in ever larger numbers. Suddenly, many began to accept Jesus as their saviour. Parents, thrilled at their teenagers being kept from trouble, began to stream into the building and ask what was available for them.

Jim decided to take some of the ex-gang members away on a weekend adventure course. He thought it would be wonderful for them to walk in the forests and spend some time away from the inner city. Going to seek permission from one family, he was met by the question, 'What about me?' from a boy's mother.

'What do you mean?' Jim responded.

'Would you not desperately need something if you lived trapped behind these four walls in this place?' she asked. Jim quickly told her she could come, he could review the sleeping arrangements later!

'What about me?' cried a voice from the sofa. A man sat there with a carrier bag full of alcohol. 'I'm his father,' he began, 'but I live round the corner with someone else. I need help, I'm an alcoholic. I carry a bag of booze like this around with me everywhere I go. I need something too. What about me?' Of course, Jim made way for him too. This became an all too familiar cry. 'What about me?'

We realised we were changed people. God had stirred our hearts. Love for the lost was a reality, love for the poor, love for the down-trodden. Prophecy after prophecy during renewal had foretold of the ministry of Jesus beginning as renewal gave way to the harvest. We were seeing this happen before our very eyes. The ministry of Jesus had begun. We were all moving out into a lost and needy world as carriers of his presence.

It is easy in a move of God to make the same mistake as the Jews awaiting the coming of their Messiah and believe the ministry of Jesus would begin with a bang on a huge triumphalistic high, ushered in on a cloud of glory. No. Jesus's ministry was unrecognised. Even John the Baptist wasn't sure if he was the promised one. Jesus didn't come as the delivering warrior-like Messiah to beat the Romans into line. He came as a servant, and went about doing good wherever he found it to do.

Our hearts burst with love for Jesus. The stony, proud,

116

patronising, zealous, ambitious hearts of two years ago had been changed into hearts of flesh carrying the heartbeat of the Father. Over and over again we heard a message from the throne room, 'The Lord hath need of you' and donkey after donkey was loosed to carry the presence of God to a needy world.

As the mothers and fathers of the street kids streamed in, so the hurting came. As the hurting came, the homeless came. As the homeless came, the needy came, the desperate came. We found we could fill the building twenty-four hours a day and never close. Our people were challenged to come and help in whichever project was running at a time suitable for them. Instead of serving the body of Christ from all over the world night after night we were serving the unchurched looking for a saviour.

Jim and Marie now began to run services for parents as well as their teenage children. They too wanted to be part of all that was going on. One of our members, Ruth, a school teacher, had begun a Kid's Club on the Bill Wilson model.[1] So many parents turned up at each Wednesday evening meeting she too began appealing for help to minister to the flood of parents coming with their children. The two women, Elaine and Linda, whose story I told earlier, began a drop-in centre and offered, along with a team of helpers, a midday meal for those with nowhere else to turn. We as a church people began to donate clothes and food. Such are the numbers flocking to this ministry we don't have any more space in the building, and we ran out of food!

Suddenly, people dressed in our own clothes began to

1. Bill Wilson leads a large work among children in New York, providing ongoing committed care.

turn up at church on Sunday. Men and women now radiant with the love of Jesus, radically saved, they were as dynamically and radically changed as Jim Richardson had been. Recently one Sunday morning, I called one man up to the platform to share about the feeding of the homeless. I thought I recognised him as one of the helpers. We were all astounded at his story, though he is only one of many.

His name is Alan and that morning he began to share how until only four months ago he was permanently unwashed, covered in cigarette ash and primarily horizontal in a haze of alcohol. Vicious with his children, he had not been allowed to see them for some time. He was a drop-out, an alcoholic no-hoper. With tears streaming down his now clean face, immaculate in his new clothes, he testified to the life-changing power of the Lord Jesus Christ. He shared how hopelessness had been transformed by an encounter with his saviour. 'I am now free,' he cried. 'Jesus means everything to me. I have a life to live.' At that moment, two little boys ran from the middle of the congregation and, falling down to his knees, he hugged them. 'These are my sons,' he wept. 'They have their father back.'

None of us could hold back our tears, and a young man of some dignity came out of his seat and bent over to comfort Alan and his children. 'Who are you?' I asked. 'I'm Tim,' he said. 'I found Jesus last week. I'm a graduate with a good degree but I couldn't get my life together. I met all these men,' and he waved his hand across a section of the congregation, 'at the hostel for the homeless. Last week I gave my life to Jesus, and I've found a reason for living. We are coming along to help at the drop-in centre and lead people to Jesus.'

Weeping and astounded, I looked out over the crowd. We were amazed that here was another river being squeezed out of the sponge we didn't even know about. Men began to lift their arms and wave back at me, glowing with their new faith. One needy man who had attended the renewal meetings at Sunderland from the outset lived in a hostel for the homeless. He was at the centre of another move of God. So many are the men finding Christ (I have to say here Herbert is in his element, Mary too!) that we are having to put on special services for them in their hostel as they learn more of Jesus and daily win others for him.

Spontaneously all over the place the needy are finding Jesus. Visitors coming to Sunderland are still turning up, but now they are witnessing first-hand the fruits of renewal, moving into mercy and mission. None of these new people have previously been churched. We are reminded constantly of the Salvation Army of old. Upon reflection, it is no wonder that the Lord broke us out of church as we knew it. We gave him his church back and he took it. Now it was going to be church his way.

During the last week we have, as a local church, ministered to three hundred of these people, the majority of whom have come in over a four-week period.

We were being pressed to free our church building for these people but where could we go? The Lord knew. We were about to experience miraculous provision.

Chapter 20

Miraculous Provision

As I pen the final words to close this book, I have at this moment the privilege of glancing up to gaze upon an exceptional landscape. Rolling hills, tall sturdy trees, horses, dogs, sunshine, as far removed from my own environment in Sunderland as I could possibly be. Here in Queensland, out of town in the bushland of Australia, things are very different. We are two British city-dwellers in an alien environment.

Large brown lizard-like creatures run up the walls and across the floors in bedrooms, lounges and anywhere else they happen to turn up. Guanas, harmless but intimidating. Spiders the size of saucers creep out from crevices you hadn't noticed and you wish they would go back again. Beautiful white parakeets screech in the trees and mice run around with abandonment. Even this morning I was quite unnerved to open the fridge door to take out a cooling drink only to glance down and meet the frozen gaze of a mouse caught in a trap at my feet!

Every day, before putting on our shoes, we remember to shake them to ensure there are no lurking red-backed spiders of which there are a profusion at the moment. Red-backs are highly poisonous spiders, and may be waiting to take a bite of unsuspecting toes. We have been careful not to swim where sea-wasps could kill us in a moment, or sharks could enjoy a fresh meal of British flesh. Of course, upon entering the water we have been careful not to be carried off by the 'rips' or currents which sweep unsuspecting tourists to their deaths. When a frog has appeared in our bedroom, jumping like an Olympic athlete we have been careful to scoop him up sensitively and lift him outside. His much larger cousin, the poisonous toad, we've left alone. Woken at dawn by a cacophony of alien sounds we realise we are in a totally different culture and it is not easy to adapt.

To make matters worse, we are living with the total embodiment of 'Crocodile Dundee'. In his spare time he wrestles snakes and has pictures to prove it. Only yesterday a rat crept up to sneak an unsolicited drink from the pool, but old 'crock' was up in a flash. Trapping the fairly large rat in the pool net, he proceeded to beat it to death with a hammer! We are certainly seeing life in all its fullness.

Though we might joke and have a great deal of fun with our hosts, precious godly people, we realise the world we inhabit in the northeast of England is totally different from their own.

Each evening as we gather around for a comforting cup of English Breakfast tea, we wait for the story from today's activities to unfold. Either the bulls' horns were cut too low, or maggots had infected the brain of the cows, rats had woken them up running across their duvet or snakes had been curled up under a pillow. We tremble! And yet, as we describe the gang violence, the theft, hatred and aggression of our own city, the same astonishment grips their features. To walk to work over broken glass, bricks and debris is unheard of for them. That rising fear as you walk through the city on a Friday or Saturday evening, they have never experienced. Two cultures, so different, so diverse have, for the last week, been living in the same house and my! Has it been fun!

That is exactly what is happening in our church at the moment. Rough men from the streets, can of lager in one hand, Bible in the other, saved only days, march in to hear about Jesus. Prostitutes or the homeless women sit down with one of our most refined ladies and learn how to make decoupage pictures while she tells them more about Jesus, and how best to work out their lives as they now follow him. A man, who has lost everything – family, friends, home, job, reason for living – after being presented with a free meal begins to draw some of the helpers and we discover a talented portrait artist. Parents, devoted to their young children, swap tips over coffee before their basic Bible study begins.

The street kids stream in after darkness, tough, plain-speaking and fierce. Yet they wrap their arms affection-ately around the sophisticated, finely spoken English teacher who is moving from Sweden to Sunderland with her husband to help us in this work. Herbert, seventy-four years of age, forty-seven of those years spent in the ministry, leads a young man with earrings and large tattoos to Jesus in a corner while his friends all whoop with delight.

Two cultures are colliding in our church each bemused by the other, yet loving each other with a passion only Christ can bring. Grace, tolerance, mercy and trust are visible everywhere.

God broke us out of our church structures and controls by disrupting our own plans with renewal services every night and didn't want us to go back to nice cosy church as we had known it. Now, church is happening all the time in all situations but never how we expected it. With a large congregation of about six hundred people and about three hundred unchurched in our now-blossoming harvest, along with continuous visitors from around the world, we desperately need more room. Jim Richardson, Elaine and Linda, Ruth and all those involved in ministry to these wonderful people desperately need us to vacate the building so they can expand these activities. They would like to see the place open night and day, and if we the congregation of Sunderland Christian Centre could find a venue, they would fill it.

Financially we were unable to see how all this could happen. Many of us had sold our homes only four years ago to put up the present building. Though it cost £550,000 to build, we have a remaining mortgage of £170,000. With no money to purchase a building, a substantial mortgage on the one we have and an influx of large groups of people who needed our financial support it seemed an impossible task. With God, however, we are reminded all things are possible. As I led the prayer meeting a few weeks ago, I was impressed to lead the people in a shout of praise, thanking God for the finances to help with all we needed.

At that very moment a businessman from Norwich and his colleague, a member of our church in Sunderland, who have a prosperous business, felt the Lord tell them to purchase a building and give it freely to us. Give it to us? We couldn't believe it. Not only that, but the building they had in mind is only yards from our present site, a former government building, so specifications are high and it consists of ten floors, each of which is the size of our present auditorium.

As the businessman told us the next day over lunch what

123

God wanted him and his colleague to do, Ken fell to his knees there and then in the restaurant and thanked God from the bottom of his heart. Because this new building is so near, we can flow with all God is doing in both buildings. We need not separate one from another. God has provided extraordinary amounts of space both for administration and practical use. The two cultures can continue to live happily as one, just as God intended it. Though as yet we do not have the finances to run the building God has provided, we have no fear. 'He will supply our every need according to his riches in glory.'

We are staggered by his goodness. On 5 June 1996 we take the keys to our new property and we thank God for the beginning of the harvest he has sent us. We plan to fill both sites with all who will come, and changed and empowered by the Holy Spirit we carry his presence into the highways and byways compelling all to come in. The harvest has begun. The Lord has provided a facility. We continue to go to those considered irredeemable. Our hearts are changed. Compassion for the lost needs to be the heartbeat of all those desiring to be carriers of the presence.

All of us who have been so deeply and profoundly challenged by the Lord during this great awakening of his Church are like Mary the young virgin, chosen by God to carry his presence in the form of his Son, Jesus Christ, saying 'Yes' to all he asks us to do. It may mean like her we could lose our reputation, our status, friends, family or even worldly wealth but like Mary faced with those eventualities we cry, 'I am the Lord's servant. May it be to me as you have said' (Luke 1:38). 2 Kings 4:1–7 recounts the story of the woman with a jar of oil. 'The wife of a man from the company of the prophets cried out to

Elisha, "Your servant my husband is dead, and you know that he revered the Lord. But now his creditor is coming to take my two boys as his slaves.'" Her husband had died, and creditors were coming for her sons, to sell them into slavery. Who could she turn to? Elisha the prophet.

All the poor woman had in her home was that jar of oil. The jar could be a symbol of the measure of the Spirit in our own lives. We are all capable of trying to get through life with only a small jar of oil. That little jar of oil was not changing the widow's circumstances or keeping her creditors away. Our own small jar of oil we are used to operating in will not change our world or our own circumstances. The little oil we have might get us to church and keep us nominally spiritual. Many pastors and preachers attempt to lead the church with only a small jar of oil. Some can preach reasonable sermons, conduct weddings and funerals, keep people happy but be ineffective in changing our world.

The prophet's advice to the woman was to bring vessels from anywhere she could find them – neighbours, friends, relatives – and then shut the door. I would like to think we could shut the door on our own plans, methodology, traditions, religion and let the oil freely flow. That little jar of oil flowed into as many vessels as would be filled. The instruction was given: 'Go and find more vessels', but there were none and the oil ceased. Perhaps some had vessels full of other necessary things, but didn't fully appreciate the value of the oil. Unless vessels were emptied of their contents, they could not be filled with oil. The same is true today. As long as we are emptied the oil will continue to flow.

The oil paid off the creditors and changed her world. God performed a miracle of multiplication and he wants to do the same today. The Father waits to multiply the measure of the Holy Spirit he is pouring out at this time. This oil is of great value. We need to be emptied of ourselves, realise a little jar of oil will not change the world. We need to bring our vessels to be filled and see our world change around us.

Today the Father cries, 'I have need of you! How will you respond?'

'When the Son of Man comes in his glory, and all the angels with him, he will sit on his throne in heavenly glory. All the nations will be gathered before him, and he will separate the people one from another as a shepherd separates the sheep from the goats. He will put the sheep on his right and the goats on his left.

'Then the King will say to those on his right, "Come, you who are blessed by my Father; take your inheritance, the kingdom prepared for you since the creation of the world. For I was hungry and you gave me something to eat, I was thirsty and you gave me something to drink, I was a stranger and you invited me in, I needed clothes and you clothed me, I was sick and you looked after me, I was in prison and you came to visit me."

'Then the righteous will answer him, "Lord, when did we see you hungry and feed you, or thirsty and give you something to drink? When did we see you a stranger and invite you in, or needing clothes and clothe you? When did we see you sick or in prison and go to visit you?"

'The King will reply, "I tell you the truth, whatever you did for one of the least of these brothers of mine, you did for me."

'Then he will say to those on his left, "Depart from

me, you who are cursed, into the eternal fire prepared for the devil and his angels. For I was hungry and you gave me nothing to eat, I was thirsty and you gave me nothing to drink, I was a stranger and you did not invite me in, I needed clothes and you did not clothe me, I was sick and in prison and you did not look after me."

'They also will answer, "Lord, when did we see you hungry or thirsty or a stranger or needing clothes or sick or in prison, and did not help you?"

'He will reply, "I tell you the truth, whatever you did not do for one of the least of these, you did not do for me."

'Then they will go away to eternal punishment, but the righteous to eternal life.' (Matthew 25:31–46)

Appendix

Since completing this book, the unfolding story surrounding the building given to us, Crown House, has been nothing short of miraculous.

Though we have experienced incredible levels of interdenominational unity, God has begun to motivate us on yet another level. Large prophetic and media related ministries from countries all over the world, including Australia and the United States of America, are coming together in that building: each with a vision for Europe. We were certain the Lord wanted us to bless other ministries, as we had been blessed, so together in unity we could be more effective for the kingdom.

Soon we will be opening the doors and, I am sure, telling you of the unfolding story.

In these wonderful days the Lord encourages us daily to dare to believe in revival. Never has there been so much spiritual activity all over the world. In Pensacola, Florida, one church has seen over 20,000 decisions for Christ in one year. In Mexico, Latin America, Asia and even China, God has gloriously begun to move.

Lord send your fire!

O God of Burning Cleansing Flame (Send the Fire)

O God of burning, cleansing flame,
Send the Fire;
Your blood-bought gift today we claim,
Send the Fire today.
Look down and see this waiting host
and send the promised Holy Ghost,
We need another Pentecost,
Send the Fire today
Send the Fire today.

God of Elijah, hear our cry:
Send the Fire;
And make us fit to live or die,
Send the Fire today
To burn up every trace of sin,
To bring the light and glory in,
The revolution now begin,
Send the Fire today
Send the Fire today.

It's Fire we want, for Fire we plead,
Send the Fire;
The Fire will meet our every need,
Send the Fire today.
For strength to always do what's right,
For grace to conquer in the fight,
For power to walk the world in white,
Send the Fire today
Send the Fire today.

To make our weak heart strong and brave,
Send the Fire;
To live, a dying world to save,
Send the Fire today.
Oh see us on Your altar lay,
We give our lives to You today,
So crown the offering now we pray,
Send the Fire today
Send the Fire today
Send the Fire today.

William Booth, adapted by Lex Loizeds
© Thank You Music. Used by Permission.